AN INSIDER CONSUMER PROTECTION GUIDE FOR INJURED PERSONS OF MOTORCYCLE COLLISIONS IN CALIFORNIA

THE CALIFORNIA Motorcycle Collision LEGAL SURVIVAL BOOK

The Injured Motorcyclists' Guide to Understanding Their Legal Rights in California

Be Proactive and Educate Yourself with Important Legal Information First!

CALIFORNIA TRIAL ATTORNEY
MARK C. BLANE, ESQ.

THE LAW OFFICES OF MARK C. BLANE, APC
T. 619.813.7955 | F. 619.946.7835 | E. MARK@BLANELAW.COM
WWW.BLANELAW.COM
CENTERSIDE TOWER I
3111 CAMINO DEL RIO N, STE. 400
SAN DIEGO, CALIFORNIA 92108

Published 2020.

Printed in the United States of America.

ISBN: 9781-1-63385-396-6

Designed and published by

Word Association Publishers
205 Fifth Avenue
Tarentum, Pennsylvania 15084

www.wordassociation.com
1.800.827.7903

"By failing to prepare, you are preparing to fail."
-Benjamin Franklin

"The books we read should be chosen with great care, that they may be, as an Egyptian king wrote over his library, 'The medicines of the soul.'"
-Oliver Wendell Holmes, Former US Supreme Court Justice

PREFACE

Any devastating injury from a preventable collision can greatly affect your life, your personal well-being, and even those close to you. This book is based on my legal experience as a California Personal Injury Attorney and Counselor of Law duly licensed by the State of California since 1999.

I have been representing injured California adults and children since that time, and my entire law practice focuses on injury cases. I truly enjoy specializing in the area of California personal injury law. It keeps me sharp and focused to specialize in one area of the law. By doing so, I stay well trained on any changes to the law, and I hone my litigation and negotiation skills with every case successfully completed. At the same time, I get the personal satisfaction of using my skill and experience to help my injured clients obtain the justice they are entitled to under the law.

A special thanks also goes to my family for supporting me and, of course, to my diligent and hard-working legal team. This includes fellow trial lawyer, Edward J. Babbitt, who joined my law firm in 2017 as an Of Counsel member, and my two paralegals Karla and Ingrid. Last, but by no means least, thanks goes to those great trial lawyers and consumer advocates who have preceded me: they have all, in some way, motivated and inspired me in my legal career; thus, I would like to thank them and everyone in my legal community who have helped all injured persons in their time of need. Keep fighting the good fight on behalf of those injured who require justice to be applied swiftly and sharply.

WHY I WROTE THIS BOOK

California boasts the most registered motorcycles than any other state with 857,677 registered with the DMV in 2018, which is 300,000 more than the next closest state's registration! In San Diego, where I practice law, there were 86,450 registered motorcycles by the end of 2019. So, this means we have a lot of people riding, and there is no legal book out there that shows how each motorcycle injury case gets exploited and taken advantage of by the defense lawyers and insurance companies.

According to the California Highway Patrol (CHP)[1], in 2017, there were almost 200,000 injuries from motor-vehicle crashes on our California freeways. On average, a fatal or injury traffic crash was reported every 3 minutes! Also, on average, 1 person was injured every 1 minute and 53 seconds as a result of a traffic crash! Of those statistics, there were 566 motorcyclist killed, and 14,148 motorcyclists injured in a freeway or street crash through-out California. With the state populated with a ton of motorcyclists, and high numbers of crashes, it makes this state a breeding ground for insurance company defense strategies and tactics.

I wrote this book to explain the defense strategies and tactics which tend to mystify a California motorcycle injury cases, and what you can do to educate yourself in case you are involved in a motorcycle collision. I want to make sure you understand your legal rights in case you or a loved one is injured by the wrong and

1. Per CHP's Internet Statewide Integrated Traffic Records System known as "SWITRS."

unsafe choices of another. The book discusses the legal rights of a person injured in a motorcycle collision – read it now, before or after you are involved in an injury producing motorcycle collision. I wanted to write this book in a way to make these California motorcycle laws easy to understand to someone who is not a lawyer or judge. However, I encourage you to call me with any questions you may have while you are reading this book, or after you have finished it. It is my belief that if you know the information presented in this book you will have a better understanding of your motorcycle collision case, and you will also know what questions you will need to ask your lawyer (if you have one) in order to help bring justice (legal closure) to your specific injury case.

You can check out more information at **www.blanelaw.com**. Learn about the laws of California, and the process when it comes to preventable motorcycle collision cases by having this powerful information first!

Mark Carleton Blane, Esq.
Attorney at Law
Email: **mark@blanelaw.com**
Specializing in Preventable Injury Cases & Insurance Claims
www.Blanelaw.com
Direct: **(619) 813-7955**

BOOK SUMMARY AND SUGGESTIONS

This book focuses on many different facets when it comes to a preventable motorcycle collision resulting in injuries in California. It includes the law, and the legal process an injured person may face. The book is divided into four parts:

- ***Protecting Your Financial Well-being;***
- ***The Safe Motorcyclist;***
- ***The Injured Motorcyclist Defense Strategy; and,***
- ***Frequently Asked Questions (FAQS).***

A basic understanding of the motorcycle insurance laws are in order in the beginning, so you know how to best protect yourself while you are out riding. This is immediately followed up by important information if you find yourself injured in a motorcycle crash – and the information relates to bodily injury and property damage claims.

I then devote an entire chapter to lane-splitting, including its history and why California allows it to be legal. It is important to understand this maneuver as it flows into how the defense will devalue your case as an injured motorcyclist.

The book moves into the top defense strategies, and tactics to devalue an injured motorcyclist claim in California. This is probably the most important information to get an understanding on how the defense frames its case against you. It starts from the very beginning when they open an injury claim file. The defense tactic are secretly employed to see how the insurance can devalue and deny liability, *whenever possible.*

Finally, the book closes on Frequently Asked Questions (FAQS) on what a motorcyclist in California should know or be aware of. I suggest starting wherever you feel you need the most information first. Regardless of where you start, I highly recommend you read **Chapter 5**, ***Defense Tactics***, at the very least. You will gain insight you never had before as seen through the eyes of an experienced lawyer who has handled many motorcycle injury cases.

Thus, this book is well suited to those who:

- Have a potential injury case for bodily injuries against a negligent party (person or persons who were not safe enough to prevent your harm);
- Want to be proactive and prepare for anything that could happen on the legal end with a motorcycle injury in California;
- Already have a lawyer and have more questions; and,
- Do not know where to start.

It could also be a useful tool for those who still have not retained legal counsel, those who suspect they may have a legal case, or for those who need specific legal information first.

My goal is to give you precise knowledge that will get you to the heart of the information quickly. I also understand that most people who get this book need this important information as soon as possible.

I suggest that you order additional copies of this book for your friends and family members, so they are able to take advantage of the valuable legal information and insight presented. If you are a California resident, the book is available for **FREE** as an **Ebook download** at **www.blanelaw.com/reports**.

Also, feel free to help yourself to other free Ebooks that are available to download on my website, and explore the many different legal videos I have produced that are about other common types of injury cases, and the legal process in California.

LEGAL DISCLAIMER

The information presented in this book should not be construed as legal advice on your given motorcycle injury case or your specific legal issue. The suggestions, descriptions of the law, legal process, the warnings, the tactics and strategies, that I provide in this book are not a substitute for consulting with or hiring an attorney. Please also remember that this book does not, in any way, infer an attorney-client relationship between my law office and you, the reader, and I cannot give you legal advice unless and until you hire me, and I have agreed in writing to accept your specific case (as required under California State Bar Attorney Ethics Rules).

Attorney Mark C. Blane is licensed in the State of California and this book is not intended to solicit clients outside of California. Many cases involving the different types of injuries persons sustain are complex and may involve an entire assortment of legal issues where the outcomes are strongly influenced by the unique facts of the individual case. For those readers who would like to consult with Attorney Mark C. Blane, Esq. directly, his contact information is via telephone at **619.813.7955,** via email at **mark@blanelaw.com**, or via the web at **www.blanelaw.com**.

CONTENTS

PART ONE: PROTECTING YOUR FINANCIAL WELL-BEING IN CASE OF A MOTORCYCLE INJURY

CHAPTER 1

UNDERSTANDING BASIC CALIFORNIA MOTORCYCLE INSURANCE COVERAGES

Before we dive into the all-important California motorcycle legal defense strategies and tactics, I want to first cover the foundation of your financial protection - and that is, your first line of protection, insurance motorcycle coverage. Deciding to purchase a motorcycle is a huge deal, and like other major purchases, the total cost will add up higher than the sticker price of the new motorcycle. Beyond sales tax and add-on parts, you will need to factor in California motorcycle insurance because you are required by law to carry it at all times. In the end, it is the most important financial decision because it will cover you for anything that could happen to you on the roadway, but only if you have the right coverages in place!

Understanding motorcycle insurance coverage is vital for you to understand which is why I devote the first chapter of this book to it. It is the foundation that will shape your motorcycle injury case. It will give you "peace of mind" while you are on the open road knowing you have yourself and any passenger covered.

Your standard Auto Insurance policy does NOT cover your Motorcycle:

For some readers, your motorcycle may not be your only form of transportation, as you may also own a truck, car, van or SUV. If true, then you already have auto insurance coverage for that other car or vehicle. That auto coverage does not cover your motorcycle. You are required by California law to have "motorcycle coverage" on your motorcycle, and not every auto insurance company offers it.

Some national brands that offer motorcycle insurance, as of the date of this writing, include: Harley Davidson Insurance, Triple A, Geico, Progressive, Allstate, Esurance, and Markel. **Buying tip:** Keep in mind that purchasing coverage from an insurance company that specializes in motorcycle insurance, *sometimes* tend to have higher rates. Like with anything, compare your options, then make your final decision. Check out the section later in this chapter where I briefly discuss obtaining motorcycle insurance discounts, *infra.*

California State MINIMAL Liability Motorcycle Insurance Coverage:

Liability insurance means coverage for when you are at fault for a collision. Like with your car, California requires the same minimal liability coverage for your motorcycle which is $15,000.00/$30,000.00/$5,000, or "15k/30k/5k." Which means you are only covered, if you are at fault for a collision, up to $15,000.00 for the death or injury of any one person in a motorcycle collision, up to $30,000.00 for the deaths or injuries of multiple people, and up to $5,000.00 for the property damage of another person's vehicle or personal property. This has been the required California minimal insurance requirements since the 1970s, and it is not much coverage should you find yourself in a motorcycle collision.

This minimal coverage requirement is extremely low. Think about it. If you are at fault for a motorcycle collision, and you carry the minimal amount for property damage, which is only $5,000.00, that amount is easily exceeded by the costs of today's damages. Afterall, $5,000.00 is really minor repair costs. If the other party has vehicle damage at $9,000.00, which is quite realistic, you will be on the hook for the difference which is $4,000.00! This could have easily been prevented by spending a few dollars more per month and carrying higher coverage.

The California law does not even require you to carry uninsured motorist coverage on your car or your motorcycle. This means that if you find yourself in a motorcycle collision, and you are not at fault, but the other person was uninsured, you may not recover anything for out-of-pocket motorcycle damage; or, even worse, your medical bills if injured! All easily preventable by having in place adequate (not minimal!) uninsured motorist coverage on your motorcycle.

What kind of motorcycle LIABILITY insurance coverage should you buy?

If you compare the motorcycle insurance quotes from the minimal California required coverage of 15k/30k/5k, and compare it to higher policy of say 100k/300k/100k, it is only a few dollars more per month, and well worth the investment to protect you and your family financially, and give you "peace of mind" while you are out on the road.

I recommend the minimum coverage to be 100k/300k/100k, and if it is within your budget, kick it up to 250k/500k or beyond. You can purchase umbrella insurance policies up to 1,000,000.00 for not that much more per year. Do the math and you will see the numbers do not differ too much. Never purchase the minimum as you will be "shooting yourself in the foot" both legally and medically later on if something happens. It is much financially wiser to budget your expenses in other areas, but not when it comes to motorcycle insurance.

What kind of UNINSURED motorcycle coverage should you buy?

DO NOT EVER WAIVE THIS COVERAGE! The biggest mistake a motorcyclist can make is to not buy uninsured motorist coverage. As we have already discussed, in addition to liability coverage going well-beyond the California state limits, you also **NEED TO HAVE uninsured motorist coverage**! This protects you financially from an irresponsible at-fault party who has low or no coverage, plain and simple. And, the uninsured motorist coverage NEEDS to match or reflect back your liability coverage. So, for example, if you have $100k/$300k/$100k for liability, you want the same amount for uninsured motorist. Uninsured motorist coverage will be triggered to protect you in case the at-fault driver has low insurance coverage or none at all.

Think about it, California has a ton of drivers, and statistically speaking, the more drivers on the roadway the more likely some are carrying low amounts of insurance or no insurance at all! I cannot stress this enough. I have seen too many injured clients over the years or get into a motorcycle collision with another party who either has low coverage or no coverage, and my client either has low uninsured motorist coverage or none at all! According to a 2017 study by the Insurance Research Council, it was reported that 1 out of every 8 drivers in the U.S. is currently uninsured. Just like we explored in liability insurance above, California only requires $15,000.00 per person and $30,000.00 per incident which will NOT BE ENOUGH to cover a motorcyclists' injuries in an auto versus motorcycle collision.

Also, because you are a motorcyclist, who do you think will usually suffer the most physical harm if you find yourself in a collision? You or the other at-fault car driver? The simple fact remains that motorcyclists tend to suffer greater injuries than people who are in the protected confines of a car with air bags. A motorcyclist is 5 times more likely to suffer more bodily injuries than a regular motorist in a 4-wheel vehicle.

So, what if you have big injuries with huge medical bills that are not covered under your health plan? Either because you did not have health insurance, or your health plan only covers certain types of medical care. It is then in your best interest to make sure you have plenty of uninsured motorist coverage on your motorcycle in case you need it for hospital bills or treatment.

California MEDICAL PAY coverage:

In fact, some motorcycle insurance companies offer "medical pay" or "medical" insurance on top of "uninsured motorist" coverage. It is like having a health plan inside of your motorcycle insurance policy, and I highly recommend it too. It will pay for things immediately that are usually not covered by your regular health plan like health insurance deductibles, co-pays, dental expenses, medical pillows, arm slings, crutches, prescriptions, home care, chiropractic, acupuncture, massage therapy, alternative health care modalities like reiki. Its power lies in its liberal coverage – it will generally apply to anything that is reasonably related to your medical care from the motorcycle collision. Adding it on to your motorcycle insurance, if available, is a great thing to do in addition to having liability and uninsured motorist coverage.

Remember, this is optional coverage, meaning California does not require it, but I highly recommend it. For example, I have seen some of my past clients have health plans that have a $2,000.00 - $10,000.00 deductible or limit, or a limit or restriction on co-pays. Why suffer with this when having medical pay under your policy will immediately cover such circumstances?

Most insurance companies offer medical pay between $1,000.00 - $25,000.00 on average. I have seen more, but they are rare. I recommend you purchase the most you can, and I would say that at least $10,000.00 in medical pay is "decent cushion." Go higher if you can. Another good thing about medical pay coverage is that it applies to both you, and your passenger, regardless of you being at fault. Remember, medical pay only applies to you and your passenger, not the at-fault party, that is what your liability coverage is for

if you are at fault for the collision. Sometimes clients get confused and think medical pay is for the other party, and it is not.
Also, having medical pay coverage gives flexibility to your motorcycle injury case in terms of helping your motorcycle injury lawyer maximize your recovery when the case settles. How? Well, your medical pay coverage contains a "reimbursement provision" which means that you have to pay back your insurance company what they paid out for your medical care under the medical pay coverage when you get a settlement from an at-fault driver. If you retain a lawyer for you motorcycle injury case, your lawyer can negotiate a reduction on what your insurance company can get paid back. Sometimes, depending on the facts of case, your lawyer can negotiate at least 33% to sometimes a full 100% waiver on paying back your insurance company. For example, if your insurance company paid out $10,000.00 in medical pay benefits for you, and your lawyer can negotiate only $5,000.00 be paid back from the settlement from the at-fault party, then your lawyer just increased your recovery by another $5,000.00! If the lawyer could receive a full waiver, then that comes to another $10,000.00! This is just one of many advantages of having an experienced motorcycle injury lawyer on your side.

Remember, you would not be able to negotiate down the medical pay yourself, without a lawyer, to the degree if you had a lawyer, because part of what your lawyer uses in the negotiation is the fact that you are paying a lawyer fee, and thus, the medical pay has a duty to make sure they are being fair by off-setting for your lawyer's expense.

COMPREHENSIVE and COLLISION Motorcycle Coverage:

Comprehensive and collision coverage mean the same thing, and it is referred to as property damage for yourself when you are at fault as well. This form of coverage will pay for the costs to repair the rider's own motorcycle in case of a collision with another vehicle or due to anything happening on the roadway from hitting road debris or even an animal. It covers for vandalization or damage by weather. It also covers theft and California is one of the highest motorcycle theft states in the Nation! If your damage is not caused by another third party, like road debris, or by you being careless, you will have to pay your deductible first before any claims are paid.

It is important to have this coverage not only for protection, but also for *control reasons*. For example, in case you are in a motorcycle collision, it is best to go ahead and have your insurance company inspect, and repair or total out your motorcycle as soon as possible. Not the at-fault party's insurance. Why? Because it gives you control in certain circumstances. If you don't have this coverage, you are dependent on the at-fault party to determine fault first, then they will inspect and repair your motorcycle. Well, it should come as no surprise that this sometimes takes time. Sometimes there is a traffic collision report and multiple witnesses, and the at-fault party does not accept fault until they have at least reviewed the traffic collision, spoken to their insured (the person they insure), and all witnesses.

While you are waiting for this to happen, your motorcycle is not getting inspected, fixed or totaled. Worse yet, sometimes your motorcycle is towed to a tow yard accruing daily tow yard fees. Those tow yard fees are your responsibility because you still have the duty to "mitigate your damages." By being proactive and having this coverage in place, you can take charge and have your insurance company handle the property damage right away, regardless of fault determination, or waiting for witness statements or the traffic collision report. You should assume this will happen in any collision, so it is recommended to have this coverage in place.

Also, I have seen injured motorcyclists not having this coverage only to find out much later the at-fault party only has minimal property damage coverage that does not cover the motorcycle repairs or replacement costs. This should be a "no-brainer" to have adequate motorcycle insurance coverage. Please see **Chapter 3** for more information on motorcycle property damage claims, *infra*.

PENALTIES for not having Motorcycle Insurance Coverage:

All motorcyclists are required to have insurance by law, and the legal and financial penalties are not worth going without it. First, your motorcycle license and registration could get suspended, and you will face tickets and fines for not being insured. Fines can range between $100.00 - $200.00 and even as high as $500.00 for repeat offenses. There are not many places on a motorcycle you can keep proof of insurance, so it is recommended to keep proof in something you take while riding, or just keep it in your personal wallet.

Without proof of insurance, your motorcycle could be impounded too, which means you will need to pay more to retrieve your motorcycle from the impound lot. And, the impound authorities will not release your motorcycle until you provide proof of motorcycle insurance. So, in the end, you will pay out more money than you would if you had motorcycle insurance in the first place.

But really, worse of all, if you are injured in a motorcycle collision, and you are not at fault, but you were without insurance, you cannot sue to recover for pain and suffering damages (also known as "non-economic damages'). You will be considered a **"Proposition 213"** which is the law that forbids your ability to go after the largest part of your injury case, which is the pain you endured and the length of time you endured it from your injuries and medical care. It includes, but is not limited to, suffering from disability, loss of consortium, and disfigurement damages. The only exception is if you are injured by a drunk driver, but that still does not justify being a "proposition 213 claimant."

As a "proposition 213 claimant," you can still go after the at-fault party for everything else like your property damage, your reasonable and necessary medical bills, and wage loss, including mileage to and from doctor visits, but that is all. Your greatest value driver is taken away from you as punishment for not being responsible enough to have liability coverage in place, even though you are not at fault for the collision. The reason alone should be the greatest motivation to make sure you have, at the very least liability coverage, in addition to the other coverages I am discussing in this chapter.

Insurance Coverage for MODIFIED Motorcycles:

Many motorcycle enthusiasts like to "trick out" or modify their bikes, but unfortunately, those modifications are not covered by your regular California motorcycle insurance. Usually these modifications are for after-market performance parts, or body augmentations made after the purchase of the motorcycle. In order to have these modifications protected, you will need to purchase additional insurance coverage for your modified motorcycle. Be sure to keep accurate written records of your modifications for insurance purposes later if damaged in a collision. Take photographs as well and keep them on your computer file.

DISCOUNTS are available for motorcycle insurance:

As with regular automobiles, there are items you can do to reduce your motorcycle insurance rate. You can qualify for discounts if you complete a motorcycle safety course or invest in any anti-theft devices for your motorcycle. There are discounts if you select a higher deductible or paying for 6-12 months coverage up front (semi-annual or annual payment) or bundling your insurance policies together. For example, bundling your home and motorcycle insurance policies under one insurance company. Most insurance companies offer discounts if you take any of the above actions.

SUMMARY of California Motorcycle Insurance Coverages:

As we reviewed in detail with this chapter, I recommend you have adequate, not minimal, coverages in the following five main areas of your motorcycle:

1. Liability;
2. Uninsured Motorist;
3. Medical Pay (if offered);
4. Comprehensive and Collision;
5. Additional coverage for any special motorcycle modifications, or after-market parts, if any.

Ideally, as discussed, I recommend at LEAST 100k/300k/100k for **both liability and uninsured motorist**, but if you can afford 250k/500k, or up to $1,000,000.00, or beyond to $2,000,000.00 with an umbrella policy, it is the best protection and peace of mind for you.

If you got this chapter down, you are going a very long way in protecting you and your family from the pitfalls of not having the right motorcycle coverage in place.

CHAPTER 2

IMPORTANT CALIFORNIA MOTORCYCLE CRASH INJURY INFORMATION

In California, both driver and passenger in a motorcycle collision can sue the other vehicle driver who caused injuries. If the motorcyclist is at fault, and was carrying a passenger, the passenger is entitled to sue the motorcyclist for injuries, if any. In order to best understand the important legal information contained in this book, it is best to start with the foundation of what you need to know in California regarding a motorcycle collision and bodily injuries.

We will cover minimal motorcycle licensing requirements, as you need to be specially licensed to drive a motorcycle in California, and then go into other issues that you need to be aware of in California if you are involved in a collision producing injuries to you and others.

California Motorcycle License Minimal Requirements:

Anyone wanting to ride a motorcycle in California must possess a valid motorcycle license at all times when riding. California issues different classes of driver licenses for operating any two-wheel vehicle (motorcycle):

> **Class M1** – This license permits operation of any two-wheeled motorcycle and all vehicles listed in Class M2.
>
> **Class M2** – This class authorizes operation of a motorized bicycle, moped, or bicycle with an attached motor.

These two classes of licenses are for people wanting to operate vehicles with only 2 wheels. However, for those who want to, the California DMV permits anyone holding a valid **Class C license**, which is the license issued for standard motor vehicle operation, to operate a motorcycle with a sidecar attached, a three-wheel motorcycle (trike), or a motorized scooter.

Applying for Your California Motorcycle License:

The process of earning a California motorcycle license depends on the age of the applicant; anyone under 21 years of age must complete additional steps before being granted a California motorcycle driver license. This is due to public safety concerns and to make sure those under 21 years of age understand what is required in order to safely ride a motorcycle on California freeways.

Process for Applicants Under 21 - Instruction Permits:

Anyone not yet 21 years old must hold an **instruction permit** for at least 6 months before applying for a motorcycle license, only if you are between ages 18-20. If you are 15 ½ to 17 years old, you need a parent or guardian to sign your paperwork. To get an instruction permit, you must take and complete the CHP approved **California Motorcyclist Safety Program (CMSP)** training course, and present evidence of the completion certificate at the local California DMV.

In addition, you also have to complete a driver license or identification card application, and provide your full legal name, Social Security number, pass a vision examination, pay the application fee, and pass a knowledge-based test. You have only 3 chances to pass the test before you are required to begin the process all over again. Once you complete these important steps, you will receive a permit, so you can hold it for at least 6 months before applying for a motorcycle license in California.

Getting Your California Motorcycle License and You're Under 21:

As discussed above, once you have held a valid instruction permit for at least 6 months, you can apply for a full California motorcycle license in California. However, in order to that, the local DMV will need:

- Evidence of your instruction permit;
- Proof of completing driver education, and training if you do not already have a regular California driver license;
- Evidence of your completion certification from the **California Motorcycle Safety Program (CMSP)** training course. Due to the fact that you have completed the CMSP training, you will not need to take a skills test. However, they may perform an observation test.

Process for Applicants Over 21:

Applications for those over 21 is much easier. Applicants over 21 may apply for a California motorcycle license without holding an instruction permit first. However, you will still be required to take either the CMSP, as described above, or pass a motorcycle driving test at the local DMV. The motorcycle driving test includes:

- A pre-trip inspection;
- Riding in different track paths properly and safely;
- Slow riding test; and,
- Gear shifting properly and safely.

Remember, the test at the DMV requires making an appointment, and providing proof of financial responsibility, so keep this in mind when you book your appointment.

To apply for your California motorcycle license, head to your local California DMV. You will be asked to provide information such as your Social Security Number, verify your identity, pass a vision exam, pass the knowledge test, have a fingerprint and photograph taken, pay the application fee, and either present your CMSP certificate or take the motorcycle driving test. No matter your age, whether you are under 21 or over 21 years of age, once you complete all the requirements, you will immediately be issued a temporary license at the DMV, and your other permanent motorcycle license will follow shortly in the mail to your home address on file.

California CHP officers investigate a motorcycle crash scene in on the I-5 in Castaic, California

What Should I do at the Motorcycle Crash Scene?

Should you find yourself in a motorcycle crash, first, if you are able, check on anyone injured. Usually, if you are a motorcyclist, it is generally you, and another person driving a car or truck that are involved in a collision. It is rare that two motorcyclists are involved in a collision. Thus, the likelihood is that you will be the one that receives the attention, especially if you are hurt. This is one of the many reasons why motorcycle collisions are unique.

Second, contact the police so a traffic collision report can be taken. If no one is injured, sometimes the police will not come to the scene. In that case, make sure you obtain the name, address, telephone number and insurance company, with a complete policy number, of the person or persons involved in the collision. Exchange of insurance information is required under California law by California **Vehicle Code Section 16025**; the only exception is for a driver who is rendered incapable of doing so because of the collision. So, if anyone refuses, call the police and report a hit-and-run.

Third, use your smart phone to take photographs of the property damage, and any information on the other parties involved. Do this especially if the police do not come out. Sometimes my clients take smart phone video of the collision scene which has proven helpful in many different ways.

Fourth, it is always best not to admit fault at crash scene, not even to the police. The reason is you may not be at fault even though it seems obvious that you may be at fault. If you do, it becomes "an admission by party opponent" and can be used against you later. It is categorized as a statement against your interest and not even a hearsay objection can keep it out of court. This is true especially if you admit fault to the police and it is recorded in the Traffic Collision Report. In California, police officers are not allowed to testify as to who was at fault in a collision, unless they witnessed the collision, but a police officer can testify that you told him or her that you were at fault. If the other driver continues to blame you for the collision, let them. Proof of your fault has to be proved later by them, and without legally required proof, the other driver is just "wasting their breath."

As a motorcyclist involved in a collision, you sometimes become the focus of being at fault because the other driver will say "that you came out of nowhere," or that you were "unsafely lane-splitting" (See **Chapter 2** on *lane-splitting*) or "speeding." It is best not to get lulled into a fault argument at the collision scene. Just focus on the injured, gather information on all the parties, and use your smart phone to take photographs and video if you are able.

If you are injured, and you are leaving the scene in an ambulance, then make sure you focus your conversation on your injuries with the emergency technicians. Usually the police officer will follow up later with you for your statement on what occurred at the hospital or the next day via telephone so they can complete their traffic collision report. If there is a police officer present, you can rest assured he or she will obtain the insurance information from all the parties involved.

I have been injured, what should I do first?

See a doctor as soon as possible! This may seem obvious, but you would be surprised how many times I speak with injured people who have not yet seen a doctor. Your medical care and your health come first, and your legal case against the at-fault person or persons comes second. Seeing a doctor right away protects you, and is used to show your damages. Ultimately, a jury or judge, if required, is the last person or group of people that determines value on your motorcycle injury case, and they will want to see, if you were injured, that you "turned heaven and earth" to get medical care. Otherwise, a defense lawyer will try to prove you were not injured by showing how there is no medical care or gaps in your medical care.

Next, let all involved insurance companies know you have been in a motorcycle collision so they can open their files and report the collision to the California DMV, if necessary (see the **SR-1 Form Filing Requirement** question below). You will then be assigned a "property damage" or "collision coverage" adjuster who will help you through the claims process. Giving a recorded statement to an insurance adjuster is not advisable until you have discussed the matter with a personal injury lawyer. This is especially true if there appears to be a dispute as to who is at fault.

How do I know if I have a motorcycle injury claim worth pursuing?

You have the legal right in California, when you are injured by another for not being safe enough, to pursue that person or persons that caused your injuries for a monetary recovery. In addition to your claim, your spouse or family member(s) may have a valid loss of consortium claim or other claim against that same person or persons.

Depending on your injuries, it may be cost effective to pursue your claim with an experienced lawyer who specializes in handling motorcycle injury cases. In order to determine this, it is best to consult with one. Remember, not every motorcycle injury case will need a lawyer, but every claim should at least get one legal consult to help determine this.

The more serious your injuries, the easier it is to see you have a claim worth pursuing. **Understand:** If you are injured by a private citizen(s) or federal government (US postal driver for example), you have up to two years, from the date of your injury, to have your claim settled or filed in court or present a federal claim. If you are injured by city or state government, you only have 6 months from the date of the injury to file your claim, or you will forever lose any legal right to obtain a monetary settlement, judgment or verdict. To this end, an experienced lawyer who specializes in motorcycle injury cases will serve your needs best to accurately answer this question.

What is the California DMV SR-1 Form Filing Requirement?

California law requires under **Vehicle Code Section 16000**, if you, as a motorcycle operator, or an operator of any vehicle, are involved in a collision which causes more than $1,000.00 in **property damage** to any person, including yourself, regardless of fault, or in which anyone, including yourself, **is injured**, no matter how slightly, you (your insurance agent or legal representative) must report the collision to the California DMV (Department of Motor Vehicles) under a DMV Report of Traffic Accident Occurring in California SR-1 Form *within 10 days following the collision.*

You can find these forms online at **www.dmv.ca.gov** or obtain them from your insurance company. An SR-1 Form must be filed whenever a collision of the above severity occurs anywhere in the State of California, even if it occurs on a private road or driveway. So, to sum up, this **SR-1 Form** filing requirement applies to you:

- Whether or not you were at fault in the collision.
- Whether or not you had the proper auto insurance.
- Whether or not your license and motorcycle or vehicle registration were up to date.
- Even if the police responded to the collision, and filed a collision report.
- Even if you called the police and notified them afterwards. (The police do not pass this information on to the DMV.)
- Even if you reported the accident to your insurance provider, and they have made a determination regarding who was

at fault (insurance companies usually will not forward your information to the DMV, either.)

The good news is the **SR-1 Form** is not difficult to complete. You must include your own contact information and motorcycle or vehicle information, including the other party's information. The purpose of filing the SR-1 Form is important. Although every driver and motorcycle rider in California is supposed to have auto insurance, some do not.

The SR-1 Form provides evidence whether or not a driver had insurance. Thus, the **SR-1 Form** helps the injured person file an uninsured motorist claim with his or her insurance, if ever necessary. So, it efficiently consolidates insurance information amongst the affected parties in case that information is needed later on.

CHAPTER 3
IMPORTANT CALIFORNIA MOTORCYCLE PROPERTY DAMAGE INFORMATION

In California, both driver and passenger in a motorcycle collision can sue the other vehicle driver who caused personal property damage. If the motorcyclist is at fault, and was carrying a passenger, the passenger is entitled to sue the motorcyclist for any personal property damage, if any. In order to best understand the important legal information contained in this book, it is best to start with the process of what you need to know in California regarding property damage in a motorcycle collision.

Who pays to get my motorcycle fixed?

Who will pay depends on ***what insurance coverage*** the other driver or drivers have in place at the time of the collision, ***your own collision coverage***, if any, and whether or not the motorcycle is a "total loss" or "repairable," among other factors.

I recommend you negotiate the repairs or total loss of your motorcycle with your own insurance coverage under any collision/comprehensive coverage you have in place on your motorcycle at that time of the collision. Why do that if I am not at fault? Because it is often times better, and faster, to go with your own insurance because your insurance will not care who is at-fault, and you will be in what is called "first party stance" with your own insurance which means they have to enact their coverages with you timely and in good faith. You will not have to wait for liability investigation that can sometimes take months depending on the facts of the collision. The other person's insurance will try to reduce your repair reward. Then, your insurance will go after the other person who is at fault for reimbursement. The only downside is that you will have to engage your deductible until the other party confirms fault. But, that is worth the trouble in my opinion given the many upsides of going through your own insurance on motorcycle repair. Sometimes, depending on the facts of the collision, your insurance company may waive your deductible, so you won't have to engage it.

Now, if you don't have collision/comprehensive coverage on your motorcycle, you will have to request that the at-fault party's insurance repair your motorcycle. This will be your only choice, and in this case, the other party's insurance will first need to determine fault. This means your total loss or repair of your motorcycle will be delayed if there is an out-standing traffic collision report, or witness statements that still need to be taken. The taking of statements from witnesses and other involved parties to determine fault may delay your repair job for several days or even weeks. This is why it is so important that you make sure you have collision/comprehensive coverage on your motorcycle so you can go through your own insurance quicker and more efficiently.

Can I get my motorcycle repaired at any body shop?

Yes, you can under current California law (**Calif. Ins. Code Section 758.5**). A list of quality body shops is available at our law office, and all you have to do is ask. You can also ask your insurance company for a list.

California law says no insurance company can require a person to have their motorcycle repaired at a specific repair shop or dealer. Moreover, the insurance company can only recommend a specific place of repair if asked.

California law requires the car insurance carrier and body shop to provide a written estimate of repair with a breakdown of the repairs with reasonable costs for "workmanlike" restoration of the motorcycle.

Can the Insurance Company force me to use "after-market" parts to repair my motorcycle?

Repair facilities are allowed to use "after-market" parts but, only under the following conditions: (a) the parts must be equal in "quality, safety, fit and performance" as original parts; (b) the insurance company must pay for any reasonable cost to modify the parts to make them safe; (c) a warranty must be provided that assures that the parts are safe for use; and (d) the parts must carry proper manufacturer identification.

Does the insurance company have to let me know if there is coverage for a rental motorcycle while mine is in the shop?

Yes. The insurance provider must fully communicate the extent of coverage for a substitute motorcycle including the daily rate and maximum number of days covered under the policy.

My motorcycle is a total loss...what will be paid for it?

What the insurance company will pay if the motorcycle is declared a total loss is determined by your motorcycle's **Fair Market Value (FMV)**, aka "actual cash value," not what you paid for the motorcycle, or what you owe on the loan. The motorcycle's FMV is what an identical motorcycle could be sold for in today's market. The insurance company usually employ third party companies to do the FMV assessment, so they are far from any bias. This company sometimes does comparisons of motorcycles within 50 miles of your zip code, and this index information is disclosed to you so you can see how FMV was determined.

Blue book sometimes does not give you complete information, and I recommend using **www.cycletrader.com** to search for the asking price of similar make and model motorcycles in your zip code area. You can also contact motorcycle dealerships to find out what price they have put on a motorcycle similar to your motorcycle. If after your research, the insurance company offers you an amount within your researched range, then I recommend you accept that offer. If not, we can try to negotiate the value upwards by showing evidence of other comparable motorcycles to the insurance company in negotiating a fair market value.

If my motorcycle is a total loss, does the insurance company have to pay for the entire value?

Yes, but if there is a lien on the motorcycle (like a bank loan), the insurance company will pay the loan first, and then, any remainder goes to the registered owner, assuming that is you.

Sometimes a motorcycle loan balance may be more than the fair market value of the motorcycle itself. This happens often with clients who get into a collision with a fully financed, brand spanking new motorcycle. As you know, with a brand-new motorcycle, once you leave the dealership lot, the fair market value of that motorcycle significantly drops down!

If you believe you may be at risk for such a situation, you should consider purchasing "gap insurance" coverage to cover the balance of the loan. Most finance deals offer gap insurance and it is proactive to purchase it for "peace of mind."

Can I get a rental motorcycle?

Yes, by law, you are entitled to be provided a rental motorcycle, or car, by that at-fault party for the time your motorcycle is being repaired or being resolved as a total loss. Or, if you don't get a rental motorcycle or car, you can claim "loss of use" of transportation during the number of days it takes for your motorcycle to be fixed or assessed a total loss. Loss of use damages are very important and often over-looked by injured motorcyclists and the at-fault insurance company.

Even if you decide to drive another motorcycle or car you own, or borrow a family or friend's motorcycle or car, you would still be entitled to "loss of use" damages as notated above. **Understand:** If you qualify for loss of use damages, you must claim it, otherwise the other insurance company will not offer it, and they may not ask you if you have loss of use damages. They usually just ask if you had a rental, and no more. If they do ask about loss of use damages, the insurance company may try to tell you that the "loss of use" period runs only from the date of loss to the date of their first settlement offer. Do not believe a word of it because you, the motorcycle owner, cannot replace the damaged motorcycle until you received the funds for settlement. So, you can usually get a few days more after the first settlement offer under the loss of use period for your loss of use damages.

I have been successful in obtaining for injured clients hundreds, and in some cases, thousands of extra dollars in those situations where resolving the motorcycle property damage claim just takes extra time.

As stated earlier, I recommend you use your own collision/comprehensive coverage under your auto insurance first, and this includes if you have any rental coverage under your policy. If you have rental insurance, you can have your insurance company set up a "direct billing" with the rental car company. Why is that advantageous? There is absolutely no out-of-pocket to you! Your deductible may take a hit, but you will get reimbursed for that deductible once the other at-fault party confirms responsibility. Otherwise, you will be forced to go through the other insurance company for the rental which usually requires you to pay for the rental first, and then get reimbursed.

What if the other driver's insurance company and I disagree on the motorcycle damages?

Your motorcycle damage claim is against the other at-fault driver(s), not their insurance company, so if the other driver's insurance company is being unreasonable, treating you unfairly, taking too much time, refusing to perform an inspection, not reimbursing for tow charges, or storage fees, then your only remedy is to file a suit against the at-fault driver(s).

If you don't have an injury motorcycle lawyer retained, and your motorcycle damages are $7,500.00 or less, then you could consider filing your action in California small claims court. If you have no collision coverage, and the other party has no liability insurance, you can then file for motorcycle damages up to $10,000.00 in California small claims court, since there was no insurance involved. However, before you proceed down this small claims legal path, it is advisable that you at least consult with a lawyer who specializes in motorcycle collisions. The reason being is sometimes, with a lawyer, your damages for your motorcycle can be combined in your bodily injury claim so you can get reimbursed for those values and costs later. I had this happen when my client did not have collision coverage for his motorcycle, and there was a policy dispute with the at-fault party. So, we combined both his property damage claim with his bodily injury claim and got both values at the same time when we eventually settled the case. This will also save you a trip for having to go down to small claims court on your own.

Can I still keep my motorcycle, even if it is deemed a "total loss?"

Yes, if you "retain salvage," you may keep the motorcycle, but you will have to accept a lesser settlement offer based on the "salvage value" of the motorcycle. This is because you are receiving a benefit, the damaged motorcycle itself. For example, if the insurance company believes the salvage value is $1,000.00, they will deduct that amount from the actual cash value of the motorcycle. And, then, you will, as a second step, have to notify the DMV that your motorcycle has been salvaged so you can receive a "salvaged title" from the DMV. Effectively, this gives notice to the world that your motorcycle is not worth much even if it was fixed.

If the motorcycle collision was my fault, or partly my fault, what do I need to know?

If you are at fault, either fully or in part, then focus your attention on the at-fault party for their portion of fault, and your own insurance company to defend you on any claims made against you for either property damage or personal injury.

For example, if you have "Property Damage Liability Protection," your insurance company will defend you against claims made by others regarding property damage. If you have "Comprehensive/Collision" coverage, then you would look to your own insurance to replace or repair your motorcycle. If you have neither of these, you may have to replace or repair the motorcycle at your own expense, or defend yourself in a legal action that may be filed against you for reimbursement.

As of the date of this writing, California law requires at least $10,000.00 in property damage coverage for property damage liability, but I advise to my clients to carry at least $50,000.00, or more, in property damage liability, and a minimum of $100,000.00/$300,000.00 in both liability and uninsured motorist coverage.

Getting back to property damage liability protection, I recommend you purchase as much as you can afford. A minor motorcycle collision on an expensive vehicle, can easily wipe out minimal coverage. Especially if that motorcycle collision caused a multiple car collision to occur. If you only have California state minimal limits of $10,000.00 for property damage, and the total damages equal $75,000.00, you will be responsible for the difference, if you are at fault for the collision(s).

Understand: Your insurance protection begins with your coverages that you have in place on your motorcycle, and if you are going to be riding on California roadways, you have to be proactive and protect yourself by having adequate coverage, and avoid getting the California state minimal limits coverage. The choice to have better insurance coverage is within your control, so take responsibility and protect yourself with it.

PART TWO: THE SAFE MOTORCYCLIST

CHAPTER 4

ALL ABOUT CALIFORNIA "LANE-SPLITTING"

Are you a safe or unsafe motorcyclist? This is an important theme to be aware of that runs throughout this book, because the defense will do their best to "paint you as an unsafe motorcyclist," *whenever possible*, and they usually do this by scrutinizing your lane-splitting skills, and whether you were doing it just prior to any collision. If they cannot do this, they will get "creative" on the rules and public images that come along with motorcycle riding. This is something you should consider while you read this book. I will get more into the details of this under Chapter 5, ***Defense Tactics***. At the very least, you should read this chapter together with Chapter 5 for incredible insight in what you will face in your motorcycle injury claim.

Motorcyclists in California must follow the same laws that apply to drivers of standard passenger vehicles, but there are some state specific laws that only apply to motorcyclists, and lane-splitting is one of them. I will get into what lane-splitting is, and what you need to know to protect yourself in a moment. But first, the reader must realize the motorcycle state specific laws are designed to protect motorcyclists, as well as others that share the roadway. In addition, the reader needs to understand the beginnings of California motorcycle culture which has influenced California lawmakers to even allow lane-splitting to be performed on its vast highway system in the first place.

All other states specifically forbid the practice of lane-splitting in their motorcycle laws. Funny enough, in recent years, about nine other states have considered legislation that would allow lane-splitting to be legalized, according to the American Motorcyclist Association. Also, in many other countries around the world in both Europe and Asia, it is legal and helps to clear up traffic jams.

Motorcyclists lane-split in Bangkok, Thailand

With California's beautiful weather, it is no wonder that motorcycle riding became popular. The impact of motorcycles in California all started about 1903 with the founding of Harley-Davidson, right after the Indian motorcycle was founded in 1901. "Motordromes" became the rage which were a mile-long oval wooden board racetracks which featured motorcycle races. The first one that was built in the United States was in Playa del Rey, California, and opened in 1910. They were steeply banked (from 20-60 degrees) with huge crowds of tens of thousands seated in grandstands above the banked track. Even early racers ran close to 100 mph. There was even an oval wooden board track (motordrome) built in what is now the center of Beverly Hills in the 1920s called the Beverly Hills Speedway.

Photograph of a classic Harley motorcycle in the Southern California desert

Thus, California has had a long tradition of motorcycle culture and enthusiasts from the founding of the Hells Angels Motorcycle Club (HAMC) in Fontana, California in 1948 to the iconic motorcycles of the California Highway Patrol which was founded in 1928. California has vast stretches of highway due to its large size, and cruising on your motorcycle down a California roadway is the classic homage to this tradition.

California is also home to one of the most robust State Park systems in the great United States of America, boasting almost 300 parks in the Golden State comprising of 1.3 million acres, and 280 miles of coastline (which is the quintessential ride that most of the world thinks of when riding down a California highway). California is also home to more than 18,000 campsites, which after a long day of riding, makes a perfect spot for motorcyclists to make a campfire and bed down for the night. Also, the famous California Highway State Route 1, built in 1934, hugs the California coast for up to 656 miles of gorgeous coastline. California has the most roads listed in the "Top 100 Motorcycle Roads" on **www.motorcycleroads.com**. Yes, it is no surprise that California has a long history of motorcycle enthusiasts.

Photograph of the iconic State Route 1 Highway running through Big Sur, California

What is California Lane-Splitting?

It is then no surprise that motorcyclists love their rides because they are easier to maneuver in congested traffic due to their smaller size in comparison to other cars and trucks on the freeway. They can find spaces that other cars cannot fit through, so it is quite easy to get to the head of the lane when necessary. They can ride between the lanes of slow-moving vehicles to avoid traffic congestion and save time. Some even feel that it is a safer practice than staying behind stopped vehicles in traffic. It also helps in traffic jams by keeping the flow of traffic moving by focusing on motorcycles to flow through slower traffic.

Riding between the lanes is called "lane-splitting" in California, and everyone always asks, especially those who are not from California on vacation here or visiting, is it legal to do in the state? Many ask this question because in most states in the United States, lane-splitting is specifically forbidden by law. Lane-splitting is considered both safe and prudent and it is sometimes called: "lane sharing, filtering, or white-lining," but refers to the process of a **motorcyclist riding between lanes of stopped or slower moving traffic, or moving between lanes to the front of traffic stopped at an intersection**. Studies have shown that this maneuver can improve motorcycle rider safety as long as riding between cars is done at a safe speed. In California, lane-splitting is 100% legal, if done safely, and the history of lane-splitting will be explained below.

A 2014 study found that a whopping 80% of California motorcyclists lane-split on the freeway, with more than half of them saying they do it "often" or "all the time." The same study found that only 60.7 percent of regular vehicle drivers knew that lane-splitting was legal. When people not familiar with the maneuver see it for the first time, they think the motorcyclist is breaking the law. The only time when the motorcyclist is actually breaking the law, is when it is being done ***unsafely***. Motorcyclists are still required to obey the speed limits and other safety rules of the road, and they can be cited for a ticket by law enforcement if they do not responsibly lane-split their motorcycles. We will talk about how to do it safely in just a bit.

A motorcyclist lane splits on a California freeway

Brief History of Lane-splitting Legal in California:

Lane-splitting on your motorcycle is a long-standing practice in the California, and California motorcyclists have done it for decades. The practice does help in keeping traffic jams to a minimum by reducing congestion points. It also prevents motorcycle engines from overheating. In fact, the practice has never been prohibited by California law! There are even California news reports dating back to the 1960s acknowledging the practice. So, traditionally it has been an acceptable practice on the California freeway.

Motorcycle riders who do the maneuver say they do it for two main reasons: speed and safety. The maneuver allows motorcycles to weave through congested traffic much more quickly than regular cars or trucks, and thereby helping with congested traffic. A

2011 study from Brussels, Belgium – where lane splitting is legal – found that if you replaced approximately 10% of vehicles on the highway with motorcycles, it may reduce the time everyone spends time in congested traffic by 40%, all owing in part to lane-splitting being performed.

Even though California motorcyclists sometimes get criticized for the practice, they say it makes them feel safer while riding. One of a motorcyclist's greatest fear is getting rear-ended on the freeway either while stationary or in motion. Since motorcycles go much faster than other vehicles on the freeway, motorcyclists are more in control and tend to pay more attention to their traffic surroundings. California motorcyclists also argue that criticism of the practice really stem from the 1/10 times a regular vehicle driver see it being done unsafely, and it is that one time that stands out in their mind instead of the other 9 times that it was done safely and the regular motorist never gave it a second thought.

Even the California Highway Patrol (CHP) are not very motivated about going after those who do it, ***especially when those who do so are lane-splitting safely***. Those motorcyclists who choose not to be careful and safe, however, may be cited by the CHP for "reckless driving" (aka "unsafe lane-splitting" under **California Vehicle Code Section 21658.1**). Thus, the issue with lane-splitting is that it is sometimes performed unsafely, and we have all seen the unsafe motorcyclist's lane-splitting recklessly on our roadways from time to time. The defense will use the image of an unsafe motorcyclist, and will try to apply it to you in your motorcycle injury case. More on defense tactics later in this book.

There are certainly different interpretations and opinions of what constitutes "safe" or "reckless/unsafe" lane-splitting. Over the years, the CHP has released guidelines to help inform motorcyclists on what safe lane-splitting requires in traffic conditions. At least this reduced the confusion among motorcyclists, so they know what was, and what was not, allowed in this type of maneuver. In 2013, The CHP put up lane-splitting guidelines, but took them down only a year later after a complaint was made to the California Office of Administrative Law because the CHP guidelines could be seen as a state law enforcement agency "establishing new law." This move drew attention from leading law experts in the State of California, who then debated over whether it is within law enforcement's duty to dictate such guidelines, without it being codified in a law, code or statute. After all, the CHP is a law *enforcement* government agency—and not a lawmaking (legislative) body, and that fact fueled the heated debate.

California Assembly Bill 51 Made Lane-splitting Legal in 2016:

After the heated debates about whether the CHP can just dictate safety guidelines on lane-splitting, in 2016, Assemblyman Bill Quirk, introduced AB51 into the State of California legislature. The bill proposed to make the practice of motorcycle lane-splitting legal, and this was signed into law by California Governor Jerry Brown. Thus, at the start of 2017 the lane-splitting practice became explicitly legal in being codified under the **California Vehicle Code 21658.1.**

The good part about the bill was that it cleared up the issue of whether or not lane-splitting was actually legal in the State of

California as opposed to a safe recommendation from the CHP. It also formally recognized the authority of the CHP over the practice of lane-splitting in California. To develop safe guidelines around lane-splitting.

The bad part, however, is that some confusion still lingers over the issue of lane-splitting itself. Why? Because the law ***did not specifically describe or define*** what it meant to split lanes on a motorcycle in California lawfully – it merely glossed over the fact that it can be done legally on California roadways.

Here is how the **California Vehicle Code Section 21658.1** governing motorcycle lane-splitting actually reads, and you will see the some of the ambiguity with it:

THE CALIFORNIA LANE-SPLITTING LAW:

21658.1. (a) For the purposes of this section, "lane-splitting" means driving a motorcycle, as defined in Section 400, **that has two wheels in contact with the ground, between rows of stopped or moving vehicles in the same lane, including on both divided and undivided streets, roads, or highways.**

(b) The Department of **the California Highway Patrol may develop educational guidelines relating to lane-splitting** in a manner that would ensure the safety of the motorcyclist and the drivers and passengers of the surrounding vehicles.

(c) In developing guidelines pursuant to this section, the department shall consult with agencies and organizations with an interest in road safety and motorcyclist behavior, including, but not limited to, all of the following:

(1) The Department of Motor Vehicles.

(2) The Department of Transportation.

(3) The Office of Traffic Safety.

(4) A motorcycle organization focused on motorcyclist safety.

(Added by Stats. 2016, Ch. 141, Sec. 1. (AB 51) Effective January 1, 2017.)

This was not an issue in the original form of the legislative Bill 51 because when it was first proposed, it included a guideline that specifically held lane-splitting motorcyclists to a speed of no more than 15 mph faster than the slower vehicles around them on the roadway. These motorcycles were also only able to go up to a maximum of 50 mph while lane-splitting on the roadway. This additional information or guidelines were specifically included in this legislative bill.

Unfortunately, these guidelines were not included in the final version of the bill that became law under the California Vehicle Code. Instead, the law contained a very general provision directing the CHP to come up with a set of guidelines that covered lane-splitting. As you can read above in the quoted Vehicle Code Section, the CHP was supposed to consult with other relevant government agencies along with respected motorcycle safety groups. (To see the exact language of the law about this matter, you can look over **Section 21658.1 of the California Vehicle Code** quoted above).

California authorized one study led by UC Berkley researchers which examined collision statistics and reports covering the period of June 2012 to August 2013 that involved lane-splitting collisions. It was discovered that 5,969 motorcycle collisions were recorded in the State of California by law enforcement officials in above-referenced time frame. These included 997 collisions that involved motorcycle lane-splitting which made up 17% of those collisions.

The CHP Lane-splitting Tips:

In response to this issue, the CHP, on September 27, 2018, provided a Press Release on **"California Lane-splitting Tips."** The

Press Release went on to say: *"Although lane-splitting is legal in California, motorcyclists are encouraged to* ***exercise extreme caution when traveling between lanes of stopped or slow-moving traffic****,"* said CHP Commissioner Warren Stanley. *"Every rider has the ultimate responsibility for their own decision making and safety."* These general safety tips are provided to assist you when riding; however, they are not guaranteed to keep you safe:

- Consider the total environment when you are lane-splitting (this includes the width of lanes, the size of surrounding vehicles, as well as current roadway, weather, and lighting conditions).
- Danger increases at greater speed differentials.
- Danger increases as overall speed increases.
- It is typically safer to split between the far-left lanes than between the other lanes of traffic.
- Try to avoid lane-splitting next to large vehicles (big rigs, buses, motorhomes, etc.).
- Riding on the shoulder is illegal; it is not considered lane-splitting.
- Be visible – Avoid remaining in the blind spots of other vehicles or lingering between vehicles.
- Help drivers see you by wearing brightly colored/reflective protective gear and using high beams during daylight hours.

The CHP Press Release went on to say: "Motorists can also do their part by sharing the road. Many motorcycle collisions are caused when other motorists simply do not see the motorcyclist. Check your mirrors and blind spots frequently, especially before changing lanes or making a turn. Be alert and courteous while sharing the road.

CHP officers will continue to enforce the laws that affect traffic safety, such as unsafe lane changes, speeding, following too close, and blocking or impeding other motorists. The CHP realizes that traffic collisions can happen to anyone, regardless of their skill level, which is why the CHP strongly encourages all riders, new and experienced, to enroll in the **California Motorcyclist Safety Program**. For more information, or to find a training site near you, visit **www.californiamotorcyclist.com**, **www.lanesplittingislegal.com** or call **1-877-RIDE-411**. The mission of the California Highway Patrol is to provide the highest level of Safety, Service, and Security."

The CHP released a brochure with the following tips:

1. **Travel at a speed that is no more than 10 miles per hour (MPH) faster than other traffic** – danger increases at higher speed differentials.

2. **It is not advisable to lane split when traffic is at 30 MPH or faster** – danger increases as overall speed increases.

3. Typically, it is more desirable to split between the #1 and #2 lanes than between other lanes.

4. Consider the total environment in which you are splitting, including the width of the lanes, size of surrounding vehicles, as well as roadway, weather, and lighting conditions.

5. Be alert and anticipate possible movements by other motorists on the road.

The CHP does acknowledge that lane-splitting can be dangerous, and they advise extreme caution should be exercised. They recommend it should not be performed by inexperienced motorcycle riders. The risk of death or serious injury during a lane-splitting collision increases as speed and speed differential increases. The CHP nicely sums up their lane-splitting advice as **The Four R's** or **"Be-Attitudes"** of lane-splitting in California:

BE REASONABLE,

BE RESPONSIBLE,

BE RESPECTFUL, and,

BE AWARE OF ALL ROADWAY AND TRAFFIC CONDITIONS.

Visit **www.lanesplittingislegal.com** for more information.

How to Lane Split Safely and Without Breaking California Law:

If you choose to practice motorcycle lane-splitting, you can eliminate most of the risk by following the suggested safety guidelines:

You should go at a speed of no more than 10 mph faster than the slower vehicles around you. This may allow you see and react to any danger around you on the road. The faster you are going down the roadway compared to the other vehicles, the greater the risk of a collision with injuries.

If the traffic around you is moving at 30 mph or more, then it's more prudent to avoid splitting lanes. Even when you are traveling at only 20 mph on a motorcycle, you'll probably need a second or two to identify a problem. During that time, you've traveled 30 to 60 feet before you even take evasive measures against any safety threat. That does not yet account for the time you need to brake and swerve around the hazard or safety concern.

Your safest lane-splitting option is to do so in between the 2 left most lanes. On the other hand, you ought to avoid splitting lanes near freeway exits and on-ramps as that is "playing with fire." That is because the cars in the 2 left most lanes may turn to provide more space for motorcycles on one side, and thereby limit the space on their other side.

Be aware of your entire surroundings, the type of traffic you are in, so you can safely judge the safety hazards of lane-splitting. Keep in mind, splitting lanes near wide trucks, attempting to go through much narrower lanes, produce more of a hazard for you.

Know the weight, size and dimensions of your particular motorcycle, so you know if you will really safely fit into a space or not. Your motorcycle may have wide handlebars that may not fit through the space you're squeezing through, or other parts that make the motorcycle unsafe in a particular space or spot.

Do not try it on roads or highways you don't really know, or travel down often, as you may come upon road imperfections that can cause you to lose control. You should instead try it only on roads that you're familiar with or travel the most on. You will also gauge the time of day where there are more or less cars on the roadway.

You should also avoid lane-splitting when you have inadequate or poor visibility. It may be too dark, bad lighting or perhaps the weather is bad, or the roadway is slick. Not only will you fail to see road safety hazards in time, but other motorists may not see you as easily either. In many car and motorcycle collisions, often the cause is that the car driver didn't see the motorcyclist in time in order to prevent the collision. If the visibility is bad for you, it is bad for all the other cars and trucks around you.

You still need to drive defensively while lane-splitting. This means you have to anticipate the actions of other motorists while traveling in a lane-split situation. Some of the other drivers on the road may be distracted or even impaired, or suffer a medical condition. You always have to be on the safe lookout for changing traffic conditions. Defensive driving goes both ways, and it also means you do not drive while you are impaired.

It's best to avoid the practice of lane-splitting if: you are not sure you can fit, you are at a toll booth, if the traffic is moving erratically or too quickly, if the visibility is poor, if you notice dangerous road hazards, and if you have to go by the side of wider vehicles like trucks and big rigs or the like. The basic safety rule is that *if you are in doubt, don't do the lane split at all.*

Avoid lane-splitting at night. Nighttime makes it harder for other vehicles to see you.

Driving a Car Around Motorcyclists:

A 2014 study found that approximately 60% of drivers on the California freeway disapprove of lane-splitting. More than half of those drivers indicated it was due to their impression that it is unsafe. The rest complained of it possibly leading to a crash with others, startling drivers, it is unfair, or they thought it was illegal. Sometimes lane-splitting can lead to road rage situations which is unfortunate. Just look on YouTube under "lane splitting road rage," and you will see a ton of videos about it.

Motorcyclist lane-splitting on the San Francisco Bay Bridge

The first thing you have to accept is that the practice of lane-splitting is legal in California, and as such, you should prepare for it to be done around you. If you are not accustomed to it, it can be quite startling. When I first moved to California back in 1995, I was surprised to see it. I grew up in Louisiana and found the practice, at first, alarming. If you are from out-of-state, check your bias against the practice at the state line as it is not your call to discourage motorcyclists from splitting lanes, and any action you may do to prevent motorcyclists from splitting lanes may not be legal. It is expressly illegal for you to open your car door to block motorcycles from passing through in between lanes (**California Vehicle Code Section 22517**). You also cannot intentionally impede or block a motorcyclist in a way that can cause them harm (**California Vehicle Code Section 22400**).

You can simply practice safe driving behavior around motorcyclists on the California roadway by doing the following:

- Before you turn or change lanes, you should first check your mirrors and blind spots for other vehicles (including motorcycles). Be alert, since motorcycles are notoriously more difficult to notice than cars. If you are on any major California freeway, you should expect and anticipate motorcyclists.

- If you are merging with traffic or changing lanes, always signal your intentions. This will help motorcyclists to anticipate your actions and take evasive measures. I have always noticed that motorcyclists tend to respond faster to my car blinkers than other drivers in cars and trucks.

- When you're travelling behind a motorcycle, allow them more space so you have, at least, 3 to 4 seconds of reaction time to whatever they may do. That should help provide them an added measure of safety to hit the brakes and swerve around an unsafe hazard in the roadway.

- If you are in the fast lane (the further most left lane) on a freeway, and you see a motorcyclist approaching and intending on lane-splitting, you can nudge over to your left a few inches to help accommodate their lane split. You sometimes will get a wave of appreciation from the motorcyclist.

We all know, traffic in California is always a problem, and it is understandable that some motorcyclists may want to save time by splitting lanes. Some of the logic for lane-splitting is the fact that is helps with traffic congestion by keeping the motorcycles going in the flow of traffic, especially during a traffic jam. It is perfectly legal for them to lane split, and it does not matter if you agree with this or not, as it is the law in California.

What does matter is that whether you are a motorcyclist or a car driver, you drive safely with proper respect for the other motorists around you – this means, the "Rule of Reciprocity" is alive and well in California. **Understand:** I depend on you to obey the safe traffic rules, and you depend on me doing the same for you. Together, we will get home safely to our loved ones.

Scientific Safety Studies on California Motorcycle Lane-Splitting:

As of the date of this writing, there are not a lot of safety studies performed on the practice of lane-splitting. So, very little scientific date exits on how safe it in fact is. A 2015 study performed by the Safe Transportation Research & Education Center at UC Berkeley found that 17% of about 6,000 motorcyclists who crashed between June 2012 and August 2013 were lane-splitting at the moment they crashed.

Per the same study, "*lane-splitting appears to be a relatively safe motorcycle riding strategy if done in traffic moving at 50 mph or less, and if the motorcyclists do not exceed the speed of other vehicles by more than 15 mph.*" The study goes on to say that its findings cannot be used to compare the overall safety of lane spitting, "*To estimate how the risk of being involved in a collision changes when motorcyclists choose to lane-split, we would require information on both the lane-splitting and non-lane-splitting riding that is done by some identifiable sample of motorcyclists. The collection of the data is fraught with problems, and the current study did not attempt to collect such data.*"

According to the National Highway Traffic Safety Administration, data shows California is in the middle when it calculates motorcyclist fatalities per 100,000 registered motorcycles compared to other states. Yet, this national data does not take into consideration other factors like the differences between state laws with helmet requirements and motorcycle riding culture.

Even with the lack of scientific studies, one thing is for sure: you must lane-split safely, and do not perform it if it means you must exceed the speed limit.

What is Motorcycle Lane-Sharing in California (how is it different from Lane-Splitting)?

As the name implies, lane sharing is when there are two motorcycles traveling in the same direction on a roadway, at the same time, while in the same lane, side-by-side. It can either be done by two motorcyclists or a motorcyclist and a passenger vehicle.

A pair of CHP officers lane-sharing on a California Highway

Lane sharing is not allowed on every roadway in the state of California, however. It is limited to bigger and wider roads, where at least two lanes head in the same direction safely. While it is technically legal in California as of the date of this writing (2020), it is considered unsafe by many riders and safety experts – the California Department of Motor Vehicles' (DMV) Motorcycle Handbook discourages the practice, saying that it is "not safe... [and that] riding between rows of stopped or moving cars in the same lane can leave [a rider] vulnerable." In spite of the DMV's dislike of the practice of lane-sharing, the legislature has not acted to make it illegal, nor do we expect them to in the near future.

PART THREE: THE MOTORCYCLE INJURY DEFENSE STRATEGY

CHAPTER 5

TOP DEFENSE TACTICS IN CALIFORNIA MOTORCYCLE CRASH CASES

To understand the defense tactics employed by the insurance company, and their battalion of defense lawyers, we have to understand what makes motorcycle injury cases ***unique*** in California, as the uniqueness is what gets exploited by the defense:

1. First, as everyone knows, a motorcycle crash can **cause serious injuries** than a typical car crash, because the motorcyclist does not have the protection of the confines of a car with seatbelts and airbags. The motorcyclist is 5 times more likely to sustain greater injury than a regular car or truck driver. Due to this uniqueness, damages tend to be higher, and there is more focus by the defense to discredit the injured motorcyclist.

2. Second, a motorcyclist is also affected in a crash by the type of clothing he or she is wearing, including the type of helmet he or she has on when the crash occurs. This plays into the defense theme, laid out above, to discredit the injured motorcyclist whenever possible. If they were not wearing everything perfect, then they are labeled as unsafe if the facts allow. If not

possible, the defense mantra is then to get creative, and still try to discredit the motorcyclist.

3. Third, not everyone is a motorcyclist. Everyone either drives or has experience driving a regular car. So, motorcycle skill level is less known or experienced by the general population. In fact, not only is California the U.S. state with the highest number of registered motorcycles, but it is also the most populous state in the U.S. overall, and motorcyclists represent 12% of all registered drivers. And, skill level and years of experience amongst motorcyclists can vary widely. This also plays into the defense theme of discrediting the injured motorcyclist, whenever possible.

4. And, finally fourth, "lane-splitting" (see **Chapter 4** on "*lane-splitting*") is legal in California, ***as long as it is executed safely***. Even though this practice is legal, a lot of people do not like it when they see it. This is the final reason that makes motorcycle collisions unique and *can affect* the legal side of a motorcycle collision through manipulating the bias of the jurors in the case. And as we have continually seen, this also plays into the defense theme of discrediting the injured motorcyclist.

Based on those four factors above, motorcycle injury cases are **unique** and thereby, **more challenging**, than a regular car-on-car collision injury case, which makes them ripe to be automatically exploited by the defense. Therefore, the issues of safety linger around each motorcycle injury case. Questions like whether or not the injured motorcyclist was speeding, safely lane-splitting and/or wearing the proper protection are reviewed and scrutinized over and over again.

Understand: Insurance defense adjusters and their defense lawyers are "counter-punchers," and their job is to "sling mud on a wall just to see what sticks" to devalue a California motorcycle injury claim in any which way they legally can. They are a business, and like any business, they have to make and guard their profits. If they can minimize the value of a motorcycle injury claim, rest assured they will do it. In fact, they are paid to do just that. Job security is one way the insurance companies control outcomes, and they do not want to pay out fair value when they do not have to, even though they will never publicly admit it.

With California motorcycle injury claims, because of their uniqueness, and challenges, the insurance companies have more defenses to play with to see what might stick with a jury or judge (the ultimate determiners of injury case value). This does not make them evil, or unfair, it just means they are doing their job so they can try to win and stay employed. In fact, I have heard other injury lawyers tell me that when it comes to a jury trial, the fact that the defense lawyer showed up at all, 80% of their job is done without delivering any argument or doing much work in the trial – just showing up. Even the famous Prussian General, Carl Von Clausewitz, in his famous book, ***"On War"*** (1832), says that being on the defense is a stronger position than attack, and litigation is very much indeed like war. Instead of steel weapons and cavalry, we use paper and the courts of law.

Although Clausewitz favored an offensive attack, if done in the way Napoleon did his victories, seizing the initiative quickly and in constant motion and speed, in the battles of Jena and Austerlitz, he also somewhat cryptically, argued that defense in war was stronger than attack (offense). Clausewitz argued that the defender has an innate aversion to losing ground, and this causes the defense to fight more tenaciously to hold on to what the defense has, and to risk more to secure it. The defense can hold the ground while seeing the attack unfold, and sensing the attacker's strategy, and then using creative counter attacks, when the time comes. This is precisely what an experienced defense attorney will do in a motorcycle injury case.

Thus, your case has to navigate the court system much like Napoleon did in his victories against the Prussians. The injury case needs speed and momentum which comes from doing the settlement demand after all medical care is acquired by the injured motorcyclist. Then, before war is declared by me, by filing a lawsuit, I counsel my injured clients that with having the settlement demand fully completed, we are in "peace talks" with the insurance company to see if a "treaty for peace" (case settlement) can be agreed upon. If we are in the position to settle a case that comes within the settlement range of the injured client's case value, then I give options to my client to either settle or file a lawsuit. If we decide to file a lawsuit, I advise as to the pros and cons, and then momentum is on our side as we have every detail on the injury, or injuries, completely documented, and we can move the case toward a trial date more confidently and efficiently. We are now in a position to counter any delay or "red herring" defenses (tactical attacks) with the court. The closer the trial date approaches; the more pressure and risk is perceived by the defense.

There are many tactics that both a defense claims adjuster, and a defense lawyer do in order to devalue a case. It usually fits in their defense mantra of deny, delay and defend. Now, the reader should be aware that the majority of defense claims adjusters and defense attorneys are hard-working people just doing their job. I always have to be on-guard for my clients. Over the years, I have narrowed the defense tactics used in motorcycle cases down to **eleven (11) main defense tactics** that are in some way designed to devalue your motorcycle injury case, and they are used at the time the injury claim is reported through trial.

With this in mind, we can now explore the different defense tactics employed by the insurance companies, and their loyal defense lawyers in defending California motorcycle injury claims:

DEFENSE TACTICS #1

The UNSAFE California Motorcyclist Defense Argument:

As mentioned earlier, if you drive anywhere in California, we have all seen the unsafe motorcyclist speeding down the highway, and cutting in-and-out of traffic, lane-splitting unsafely, and sometimes surprising motorists with their noise, agility and high rate of speed. Fortunately, the unsafe motorcyclist is in the minority of all motorcyclists. The fact remains, most California motorcyclists are safe, and law-abiding citizens. As with anything in life, most people remember the "bad apples" more, as opposed to the "good apples."

Thus, the first thing an insurance company is going to want to do on your motorcycle injury case is to figure out if they can "paint you" as one of those "unsafe motorcycle riders" on our highways. They first examine the type of motorcycle you had in the collision, and then the type of motorcyclist you are. Yes, it usually gets scrutinized in that order. I first hear about the motorcycle, whether it was a sport bike or not, or what kind of stickers it had, and then about the experience level my client had as a motorcyclist or what my client was doing as a motorcyclist in the collision itself. I have heard it all.

For example, if you are involved in a motorcycle collision, the first question to be analyzed is, what kind of motorcycle did you have? Was it a "crotch-rocket," "standard bike," "cruiser," "chopper," "bobber," "touring bike," "sport bike," "motorized scooter," "moped," or "off-road motorbike?" Believe it or not, there is an inherent "biased hierarchy" on what most people would consider more unsafe just by looking at the kind or type of motorcycle involved in the collision. I have had focus groups assume my client was speeding by just looking at a photograph of the motorcycle!

Most people consider a "crotch rocket" motorcycle either the most unsafe motorcyclist out there on the roadway today, and, therefore, he or she must be the kind of person who is crazy enough to even ride it. This type of motorcycle requires the rider to assume a "Z" position with the body leaning forward onto the bike in order to reduce wind drag. A good defense lawyer can try to link in this inherent bias of this being an unsafe motorcycle (thus, unsafe motorcyclist) in the minds of jurors at trial, and likewise, a good claims adjuster will set that impression early in the claim file when the claim is first reported. I have heard that adjusters at some insurance companies are ordered to always look for fault when it comes to a motorcycle collision injury, especially on sport type motorcycles. If there are no overt facts to assert that, then they are to be creative and come up with one!

I had a motorcycle injury case where my client was in the Navy and he was riding a Triumph brand "crotch rocket" type of motorcycle with a "skull and bones symbolized by patched eye pirate" on the front plaque near the windshield and the handle bars (see photograph of it below so you get an idea):

Photograph from actual injury case I filed in San Diego Superior Court in 2017.

Although my client was following the safe driving rules at the time of the crash, the defense lawyer alleged my client was unsafely lane-splitting just before the crash. I even took the video deposition of a credible witness who was behind my client on the roadway indicating he was not lane-splitting at the time of the collision. The defense still took the position prior to trial that lane-splitting "may" have still occurred because they knew they can always toy with idea of it possibly happening just to play in the inherent bias that some people have even though they swear they will be fair and impartial as a juror. It is part of human nature, and if you have been injured on your motorcycle by another person on the roadway, you should be aware of this inherent bias. In a nutshell, the "safer your motorcycle looks," the better for your injury case.

After the type of motorcycle is scrutinized by the defense, they then focus on **YOU**, ***as the motorcyclist***. There will be many questions running through the minds of the people reviewing your file at the insurance company to see if they can devalue it. Defense oriented questions like the following:

1. *What kind of witness will you make for yourself and your injuries?*
2. *Are you a* ***safe-motorcyclist****, and how do we prove you are safe?*
3. *Do you lane-split, and if so, how often?*
4. *Were you safely lane-splitting at the time of the collision?*
5. *What is your riding skill level?*
6. *How many prior motorcycle collisions have you experienced?*
7. *How many years have you been riding, and how are you on motorcycle safety?*
8. *Did you have proper riding gear on, and if not, why not?*
9. *What could you have done, as the injured motorcyclist, to prevent the collision?*
10. *Were you over-weight or considered obese that this may have contributed to motorcycle balance issues?*
11. *Did you over-treat your injuries, or take too many pain killers?*

12. *Did you use alternative care not prescribed by your primary care physician like acupuncture, naturopathy or chiropractic?*

13. *Was there damage to your motorcycle?*

14. *How were you injured if you were not thrown off of your motorcycle?*

These questions, and many more too numerous to list here, represent the defense focus when it comes to these types of cases, and it all starts as soon as the injury claim is reported.

When I get a new motorcycle injury case, I immediately have my client *describe to me how they are a safe motorcyclist.* Sometimes my clients tell me they never ride their motorcycle at night, or while raining, or they ride just on the weekends, and not every single day; or, they never ride with passengers. In my Navy case I spoke about above, my client actually taught motorcycle safety for safely riding motorcycles on the San Diego Navy Base. So, I obtained evidence of his safety training certificates and completed safety training courses. He had many different ones, and sent them all over to the defense lawyer letting her know that she will be dealing with a *safe motorcyclist*, not an unsafe one, at trial.

I was able to frame my argument that my injured client was not only defending our country at the time of the motorcycle collision (he was active duty Navy), but he was also in charge of motorcycle safety for all motorcyclists at the San Diego Naval Base. This is evidence, and it is part of my job advocating my client's injury position. Sometimes my clients have had safety training that goes well beyond what is required by the California

DMV, like what happened in my Navy case. If you are reading this, and you are an avid rider, it would be a good investment to collect safety motorcycle trainings for your records now just in case it is ever needed in the future. At the very least, it will make you a much safer motorcyclist.

Beyond safety training certificates, training, and skill experience, if needed, we can also utilize friends, family members or work colleagues to testify that an injured motorcyclist is a safe motorcyclist. If my client belongs to a riding club, we can use witnesses from that organization too.

We can also use witnesses who are present at the time of the collision, like in my Navy case above. In that case, I obtained witness deposition testimony that my client was being safe at the time of the crash, and not unsafely lane-splitting. I always want the claims adjuster and defense lawyer to see my injured client as the exception to the "bad apples" on the roadway. Credibility goes a long way in any injury case, but it is especially true in motorcycle injury cases. Remember, an injured motorcyclist has the burden of proof, and the more we can deliver on that proof that better for the injury case.

DEFENSE TACTICS #2

The Gap in Medical Care Defense Argument:

Seek immediate medical attention as soon as possible with competent medical care! By seeking medical attention immediately, you are able to get treated by medical professionals that can document your injuries, develop a medical treatment plan, and you are *protecting your health* (well-being). Moreover, you are protecting yourself *legally!* If you do not seek medical treatment for your injuries, the at-fault driver or drivers, and his/her or their insurance companies may claim that your injuries were not serious or that you were not injured in the collision – they use any delay in medical care to make this argument. By obtaining professional medical treatment, your medical records will document the serious nature of your injuries, and provide an excellent foundation for future medical care in case your injuries become worse.

Understand: The jury or judge, who will be the ultimate decider of the value of your injury case (if your case does not settle before), will want to see that you "turned heaven and earth" to get medical attention. Why? Because a defense lawyer will argue a person who is injured normally gets medical care right away, and does not wait. Arguing this just plays into an inherent bias most people feel. It is used to chip away value on your injury case in order to defend your case.

So, do yourself a favor, and do not allow the defense to take power and value in your injury case by simply getting medical care right away and following the treatment plan without gaps in medical care. If you do not have health insurance, you should definitely speak to an experienced lawyer who specializes in motorcycle injury cases so that he or she can help you get medical care in lieu of health insurance.

DEFENSE TACTICS #3

The Prior Injury or Medical Condition Defense Argument:

Under California law, if you have a pre-existing medical condition or injury that is made worse by the motorcycle collision, then you can still get compensation for the prior injury or medical condition that was aggravated. However, if you do not have the proper medical documentation to show this, the defense will argue that you had the injury before, and it was not made worse.

I always take the position that a prior injury or medical condition will help your injury case because it explains your injury, and at times, why your care takes longer to heal. The key is to make sure your doctors properly document this aggravated medical condition, and they are able to express a medical opinion, within reasonable medical certainty, that your prior medical condition is made worse after the collision. An experienced lawyer who specializes in handling motorcycle injuries, can make sure you get the proper medical documentation for your motorcycle injury case.

It is important to have proper medical documentation for your injuries, otherwise you will not be able to claim the aggravation damages, and it may look like you are trying to *overreach* on the value of your injury claim(s).

DEFENSE TACTICS #4

The "Stipulated Defense" Argument:

This is a very common defense tactic used by the defense just before trial. Even most experienced lawyers are not aware of this tactic, and how it can impact their case at trial. This defense tactic occurs when the facts show the injured motorcyclist is 100% not at-fault, so there is no possibility of the defense blaming part of the injury producing collision on the injured party (plaintiff) to the jury. The defense will ask me if "we can stipulate to liability or fault" so the court is aware that this injury case really comes down to damages. I always decline the defense offer.

My strategic position is the defense "can admit to fault" all they want to the jury, but I am not going to "stipulate" to it because what the defense is really trying to do is covertly divide and cut off facts *of how the motorcycle collision occurred* so the jury will never hear it, and thereby to look repentant and "sorry" in front of the jury in order to gather sympathy points; to feign that they are being reasonable, and it is the injured motorcyclist who is not being reasonable.

The funny thing is, I have never had an at-fault party apologize to my client, and sometimes the defense lawyer does not admit fault until the eve of trial. This is known as "fake repentance." True repentance means you do three things:

1. **Admit you did something wrong**;
2. **Apologize**; and,
3. **Make it right** (pay for the damages), and give assurances that it does not happen again (deterrence).

We teach our children this simple three-part concept when they break a neighbor's window with a baseball. Merely admitting you're at fault only satisfies item one, and completely ignores items two and three, so it is fake, or a "red herring" argument designed to make it seem like they are paying for it and making sure it will not happen again.

Understand: If I "stipulate to fault" (formally agree the defense is at-fault) with the defense, which I never do, then the defense can object to the important facts about how the collision occurred just before and just after the collision. Our jobs as injury lawyers is to not only get our clients compensated for their pain and suffering and medical bills under the law, but also to deter or make sure the safety violations the at-fault party chose to do on the day my client was injured, *do not occur again by them or anyone else.* To this end goal, if the jury never hears about those important facts, the importance of the safety rule violations that led to the injury(ies), the jury does not know or consider the *degree of harm* in which they are preventing through their jury verdict, when the time comes for jury deliberation.

Just before a motorcycle injury trial, myself and the defense lawyer will have a court hearing called a *Trial Readiness Hearing* to speak with the judge assigned in the case, and let him or her know we are ready for trial among other procedural matters. Sometimes in these hearings, I hear the defense say that he or she has "stipulated to fault," and I have to quickly point out to the judge, that most respectfully, that is not the case. A stipulation requires a formal agreement between the parties, usually signed and presented to the judge; a formal agreement that never occurred with me. The defense may admit to fault, but I am not going to stipulate to it so they can avoid testifying on the facts of the collision itself, something the jury deserves to hear so they can properly do their job, and make the trial a fair fight. I remind the judge that one of the purposes of injury tort law is to "promote safety and ***deter unreasonable conduct***...one of the purposes of tort law is ***to deter future harms,***" per the legal authority found in *Foley V. Interactive Data Corp.* 47 Cal.3d 654, 682 (1988), and *Burgess v. Superior Court*, 2 Cal. 4th 1064, 1080 (1992), among many other California cases.

When you break out a family boardgame, what is the first question that the players, especially kids, ask? They ask about the rules of the game! They have to know this in order to play and make thoughtful decisions on strategy and potential outcomes. The jury should also know all the facts of the collision, including the safety rules that were violated, in the motorcycle crash. Afterall, the jury needs to know what safety rules they are enforcing through their collective jury verdict. The defense position would prefer to hide this from the jury. Why remind the jury of the harm the safety rules are designed to prevent? Rather, they do not want to focus on what occurred. The defense wants to keep attention on what the injured motorcyclist did with their medical care. They do not like any attention on their client, the at-fault party, and why the at-fault driver chose to violate safety rules of the road that would have prevented the injury from even occurring. I keep the focus on the at-fault party from start to finish, and keep reminding the jury about the safe rule violations the at-fault party chose to do.

So, the stipulated defense argument is used to confuse and disarm judges, as many judges are not aware that part of the purposes in California tort law is to *deter future harms*. Most defense lawyers are also not aware that the California tort law is to deter future harms that that I am explaining in this book. If a judge agrees with the defense, then aspects of the safety rule violation(s) are taken away. Of course, all is not lost if this occurs. Arguing against "stipulated fault" by the defense is not taking punitive position against the at-fault party at all, but rather a lawful position in which an injured party has the full right and range to argue, by current law. Most lawyers and judges have forgotten that one of the aspects of California tort law is to deter wrong behavior from re-occurring, and years and years of defense conditioning has made this position I describe new and novel, when in fact, it has been in the law since California developed its State Constitution and court system. In fact, every state court in the United States supports this tort law view by including some language of future deterrence in tort injury cases, including the United States Supreme Court.

DEFENSE TACTICS #5

Taking Unfair Advantage of the Unrepresented Injured Motorcyclist:

"Unrepresented" here means *without a retained experienced lawyer that specializes in motorcycle injuries* helping you in your injury case. Once the insurance company knows you do not have a lawyer, they will start doing things that take away from your injury case. Now, first, you must understand, not every motorcycle injury case will necessarily need a lawyer who specializes in motorcycle injuries because the injuries may not be serious enough to the degree that it would be cost-effective to retain a lawyer. However, every motorcycle injury, no matter how minor, should at least have a consult with an experienced lawyer who specializes in motorcycle injuries to determine the need.

The insurance company will flag the file as "unrepresented." Now, an experienced claims adjuster will do whatever it takes to convince the injured party they do not need a lawyer, even though this is against the California insurance rules. So, they do so very subtly so they do not appear to be violating those rules.

The insurance company knows that you do not handle these cases every day, and more than likely, you do not know the true value of your case. The insurance company knows you are emotionally involved since you do not have a legal advocate on your side, so you are more prone to over-react emotionally on certain items, or concede your power on other matters, and then give an unneeded recorded statement that may not be in your best interest. They do this to size you up so they can defend the injury claim for their file. They insist to take your recorded statement so you commit to a version of the story of what happened and your injuries, yet it is dangerous for two main reasons:

First, they will try to manipulate you into describing the collision in a way that puts fault into question, or diminishes your damages and injuries. This will be used against you if facts change after the statement was taken, even if it is years later. Second, when you give the statement, it is possible that not all of your injuries have appeared, or you had a prior injury that was aggravated. So, you may say something that gives them a foundation to say you were not that injured, or if your injuries get worse, the insurance will claim, the injury(ies) was due to the prior injury(ies) and not the collision. Thus, in the recorded statement you may say something that does not help your legal cause, and it can show the adjuster that your medical care is disorganized, or not properly documented.

Without having an experienced lawyer who specializes in handling motorcycle injuries, you will be asked to sign a medical records release so the insurance company can obtain your medical and employment records. They then send those records to a specialist (who works for the insurance company) to review and give an opinion on whether you were injured, and the medical care was reasonable. This also applies to any wage loss claim. As can be expected, the specialist will often find there were no injuries or limit the injuries caused by the collision. Also, the records release usually contains language that goes beyond what the insurance company is really entitled to review so they can take advantage of the information they obtain.

Continuing with the injury claim without a lawyer causes precious time to be lost because in most cases in California, the motorcycle injury claim has to be settled or filed in court within the two years from the date of injury. The insurance company then seizes on these conditions to low-ball the settlement offer, and entice the unrepresented injured motorcyclist, by causally reminding them they do not have to pay lawyer fees, or any other discreet communication to dissuade an injured motorcyclist from retaining a lawyer.

Understand: If your motorcycle injury case is not to the degree that it makes it cost effective to use a lawyer, I, or any competent motorcycle injury lawyer will be the first to tell you. However, if your case has extensive hospitalization, chiropractic or physical therapy, pain management visits, ligament, nerve or bone injury, or even surgery, your legal needs are best served by retaining an experienced lawyer who specializes in handling motorcycle injuries as possible so your file is never flagged as being "unrepresented."

DEFENSE TACTICS #6

The Use of the word "Accident" instead of "Preventable Motorcycle Collision":

Motorcycle collisions are not "accidents" as there is always a choice with a driver to obey or disobey the safe driving rules of the road. This powerful concept is embedded in the training and knowledge of our very own **California Highway Patrol (CHP)** who see the safe driving rule violations every day. The CHP do not call their Traffic Collision Report a Traffic "Accident" Report, in the same vein that one does not call a plane crash, a "plane accident," or a crane collapse, a "crane accident." Even the California DMV Motorcycle Handbook on page 13 teaches the simple concept that collisions are not accidents as follows:

"Accident" *implies an unforeseen event that occurs without anyone's fault or negligence. Most often in traffic, this is not the case. In fact, most people involved in a collision can usually claim some* ***responsibility*** *for what takes place.*

I took the deposition of a CHP officer who agreed with the above, and was well aware as to why traffic accidents are called collisions. In fact, you can view a snippet of that deposition on my YouTube channel under "Deposition Snippets" with the title: "Traffic Collisions are not "Accidents," they are a "Choice." The word "accident" infers the collision or incident was completely unavoidable, and the defense lawyers love using the word in negotiations, and trial. A true accident lacks the element of intent. As an example, a baby in highchair that is trying to eat and accidentally knocks down his or her food is an accident as the baby did not have the ability to have intent in the form of a choice. It was just an accident that he or she knocked down the food on the floor.

The simple truth is, the word "collision" is both accurate and powerful by showing the violation was a *preventable consequence.* In fact, lawyers who represent injured people in motorcycle collisions should get rid of the word "accident" in their vocabulary, and replace it with **"preventable motorcycle collision,"** because that is exactly what it is. If it is predictable, then it is preventable, i.e., avoidable, plain and simple. The defense loves nothing better but to dress up your motorcycle injury as an "accident." Their insured "did not mean to do it." They will mention this word as many times in front of the jury as they can, and I will use the other word and point out the fact that they used "accident" throughout the trial. One example is, Defendants made the decision to text while driving, etc.

Understand: Prevention of a motorcycle collision always begins and ends with the safe driving choices one makes on our roadways, and it is always a choice, not an "accident." The distinction is important because it is what protects all of us on the road.

DEFENSE TACTICS #7

The California Defense Medical Exam:

Under California law, pursuant to **California Code of Civil Procedure Section 2032**, a defense lawyer may have a defense doctor examine the injured motorcyclist prior to trial. Remember how I said that just having a defense lawyer sit at the defense table at trial, about 75% of their job is complete without having to make an argument? Well, when they pay a defense doctor to testify you were not that injured, or you over-treated, it makes up for the remaining 25%. The law allows this so there is a counter argument to your doctor's medical conclusion so the jury can make a decision. With this in mind, approximately 90% of the time the defense doctor report favors the defense, and only 10% of the time does it favor the injured motorcyclist or is fairly neutral. When it favors my client, sometimes I can use the defense expert as my expert for my client at trial, if it goes that far. Most of time, if the defense expert favors my client, a settlement before trial comes about.

In order to attack a defense doctor at trial, it has to be done respectfully and it is best to take the foundation away from their medical conclusion or opinions, or to attack the credibility of it. This can be done a number of ways, but usually it is done in a pre-trial deposition with your medical expert's medical conclusion. It is just another reason why your motorcycle injury case is like a war between medical experts.

Most of the time, these "hired defense guns" are used repeatedly by the defense and are biased so they keep getting named and paid as medical experts in trial. The doctors are repeatedly used by the defense and their names become familiar to the injury lawyers like me. It is a crap shoot as to what kind of medical report the defense doctor will write up, but it can make or break the case in terms of a settlement before trial.

Understand: It is definitely a defense tactic to be aware of, and if you are my client, I will attend the defense medical exam with you and often times record on a digital audio recorder, in addition to preparing you for the exam ahead of time. Special rules apply in a defense medical exam and you should definitely have an experienced lawyer who handles motorcycle injuries on your side.

DEFENSE TACTICS #8

The Secret Video Surveillance:

Insurance companies use covert video surveillance more and more to try to undermine the existence of injuries. They will video record you with a private investigator hiding in cars or vans when you go shopping, run errands, go to the gym, and to try and catch you in inaccuracies about your injuries. If they cannot catch any inaccuracies or inconsistencies about the extent of your injuries, then they will use the surveillance to prove that you were not limited by your injuries.

In order to confirm you have been videotaped in your injury case, I have to request it from the defense, just prior to trial, to see if they paid for it to be done. If they did, they have to turn over the video to me so I can view it, and depose their investigator in a deposition, if necessary, so that we are prepared for it should the case proceed to a jury. There are ways of possibly keeping it out of trial, but should it come into a jury trial, depending on what it shows, it can blow up in the defense's face. First of all, if it shows nothing, then the invasion of privacy is much stronger, and it will anger the jurors. Second of all, if it shows anything, it better be good, or it will anger the jurors even more. Third, the video may show something my client did, like play with his kids at the park, but the video did not show the price he had to pay later that day or the next day by making that choice. Then, that too could anger the jurors.

Understand: The point being is this defense tactic is double-edged sword, and the defense needs to cautiously wield it if they are going to do it.

DEFENSE TACTICS #9

The Lack of *Before-and-After Witnesses* Defense Argument:

At trial, if the plaintiff lawyer does not call any witnesses that knew the injured motorcyclist before-and-after the collision, the defense can use this during closing arguments. These before-and-after witnesses are either friends, family members, people in the community, or work colleagues of the injured, to testify as to *how the motorcycle collision affected the injured person physically and emotionally*. They are called "before and after witnesses" because they knew the injured motorcyclist both before and after the collision that produced the injuries. They are also sometimes called "vignette witnesses," and "damage witnesses."

Thus, this tactic would never occur with my injured motorcyclists, because I always, I mean always, find witnesses to testify about how the collision affected the life of my client. I never give the defense the chance to make this argument by saying *"where are all the members of the community that know 'Mr. or Mrs. XYZ' to tell you what they have been through with their supposed injuries? This is trial, and this is their chance to prove their damages to you, and they have brought no one here but their biased doctor."* I actually heard a defense lawyer make this argument to a jury years ago watching a colleague's injury trial, and I vowed that I will never be in that position with my injured client at trial.

Understand: I usually like to bring *at least* three, or more, such witnesses. The more the better as sometimes trial dates get pushed back last minute and not everyone can attend the court date for their testimony. It is unwise to bring no such witnesses as you will get this defense tactic argued to the jury for sure.

DEFENSE TACTICS #10

The Low Visible Damage to the Motorcycle Defense Argument:

The defense claims that having no motorcycle damage means there is no bio-mechanically force to cause injury. Sometimes an insurance company will go so far as to deny the injury claim in the beginning, without reviewing any medical records, forcing the injury party to file a lawsuit.

In such cases, both sides have to retain a collision reconstructionist and bio-mechanical engineer to prove their cause. If my client has a pre-existing medical condition that is made worse, then that fact alone can help explain why not much force was needed to cause injury. If you have a pre-existing injury or medical condition made worse from someone not being careful enough on the roadway that led to your motorcycle collision, no matter how minor the property damage, you have the legal right for full compensation that includes the aggravation of the older medical issue(s). The key to that is to have credible medical documentation and opinions from your doctor that your prior medical issue was aggravated. Without the medical records showing the aggravation, the defense will prevail on the side that you are not injured.

DEFENSE TACTICS #11

The Motorcyclist was not thrown from his Motorcycle Defense Argument:

Closely related to the low visible property damage defense argument (please see **Defense Tactics #10** above) is this defense, and it goes like this: since the motorcyclist was not thrown off their motorcycle, they could not have been seriously injured. You cannot "pigeonhole" every case where the motorcyclist does not fall from his or her motorcycle after a collision as absolute proof that the injury was minor, but the defense will use it in their arsenal of defense tactics whenever they can.

I have a case right now where my client was rear-ended on his motorcycle by a truck owned by the Department of the Navy. There is minimal damage to his motorcycle, and he did not fall down to the ground. Yet, he injured a weak shoulder that led to a rotator cuff diagnosis and surgery. In this case, I filed a federal claim with the Department of the Navy to include this aggravation of a prior injury.

So, this too is a "defense smoke screen" position designed to get into the inherent bias of any juror at time of trial. Remember, the defense slings whatever mud they can onto the wall to see what might stick to devalue your motorcycle injury case.

CHAPTER 6

THE SIX BIGGEST MISTAKES THAT WILL RUIN YOUR CALIFORNIA MOTORCYCLE INJURY CASE

Sometimes, people do not feel that they need to pursue a motorcycle injury case right away with a lawyer. They may wait for the police report, and they may believe what the insurance company is telling them – *we will compensate you fairly*. So, whether or not you are represented by an experienced lawyer who handles motorcycle injury(ies) or not, here are the six biggest mistakes that you need to avoid to make sure that you protect your legal rights, and maximize your recovery in California for a motorcycle injury, in which you are legally entitled:

1. **Not getting medical care right away, and then, when getting medical care, not maintaining consistent medical care.**

Seek immediate medical attention as soon as possible with competent medical care, and avoid getting yourself into "gaps" in your medical care! As mentioned above in the prior Chapter, **Top Defense Tactics,** by seeking medical attention immediately, you are able to get treated by medical professionals that can document your injuries, develop a medical treatment plan, and you protect your health (well-being). Moreover, you protect yourself legally too!

2. **If there is no traffic collision report, not obtaining the name and address of the at-fault party, and any witnesses, as soon as possible.**

Obtaining the name and address of the at-fault party, and any witnesses, is very important as some people panic or become forgetful after a motorcycle collision. If there is no traffic officer responding, you must obtain the information yourself immediately because it can be very hard to track down the at-fault party or parties, and any reliable witnesses to a motorcycle collision at a later date or time. It is very common for people to move and relocate frequently, and it is important to obtain reliable contact information at, or shortly after, the time of the motorcycle collision. Keep in mind, if you wait too long, witnesses may not be cooperative or may not have an accurate memory of the collision.

Take advantage of technology – nowadays, most people have a smart phone with a good camera, and most smart phones have video mode as well. Make sure you take pictures of driver's license information, and do the same with any and all witnesses. Getting information, as explained above, is very important and key in order to make sure you protect your legal rights to a future recovery.

3. **Not taking photos of any bruising or cuts, scrapes or wounds from road abrasion type injuries.**

Since this book is focusing on motorcycle injuries, the odds of obtaining bruising and road abrasion type injuries are quite high.

Remember, take photos right away, if you decide to take photos later on, the wound or the mark could heal without you realizing it, and sometimes injury photos taken soon after the collision show more details of the wound. Our law firm often hires, if necessary, a professional photographer to take pictures of the wounds at a later date after the scars have reach their maximum healing – with professional pictures, lighting is key and a good photographer can document more scarring (how the wound heals up and appears).

4. Caution: Meeting with the at-fault party's insurance claims adjuster or investigator, and giving a recorded statement.

Often times, injured people are quickly contacted by the at fault insurance company claims adjuster or their investigator. They arrange to meet with that person before hiring or even speaking with a lawyer. The adjusters and investigators often try to get you to make statements that damage your own motorcycle injury case and ask you to sign papers that will give away your rights and release them from paying any settlement in the future – (please also see **Defense Tactics #5** – **Taking Unfair Advantage of the Unrepresented Injured Motorcyclist** where I discuss the recorded statement, *above*)

It is never a good idea to meet with the insurance adjuster or investigator before contacting an experienced lawyer who handles motorcycle injury(ies). The only narrow "possible" exception is if there is no visible damage to the motorcycle and no injuries requiring medical care. Those rare collisions may be resolved without a lawyer, but I always advise you should meet an experienced lawyer who handles motorcycle injury(ies) first, no matter how minor the damages are, just to make sure you are doing everything possible to protect your legal rights to the motorcycle collision.

Also, if you give a recorded statement, and there is a traffic collision report, you are giving the at-fault party "two bites at the apple" to try and devalue your case, because, you more than likely, already gave your statement when the police officer asked you questions and recorded that in the traffic collision report. Moreover, you are never given the right to take the recorded statement of the at-fault party, unless you hire an experienced lawyer and are involved in a lawsuit for your injuries. Why give the insurance company information they don't really need, that can only increase the likelihood of it being used against you later?

5. Do not accept a quick settlement from the insurance company on your own!

There are many insurance companies out there that will try to pay you a quick settlement before you speak with an experienced lawyer. They do this for several reasons and none of them are in your best interest: First, they want you to accept less than the true value of your motorcycle injury case, and have you release them from paying any other settlement in the future. This benefits them, not you!

Second, they want you to sign away your rights before you know how serious your injuries are, how long they will take to heal, and if future medical treatment is needed – and do not be tricked when they say they pay for future medical care where they put in a close date at some future time. This type of settlement talk is misleading and only benefits the insurance companies, not you! Often times, they do not inform you of your rights to pursue or seek other damages on top of the normal negligent damages that you are rightfully entitled to under California law. You have to be careful here, and not do something that can hurt your legal case in its entirety!

6. Contacting and meeting a lawyer without experience in California motorcycle injury cases.

There are many attorneys out there that will tell you that they can handle your motorcycle injury case, but do not have the legal expertise necessary to get the best result for your case. When you hire an attorney, who has valuable legal experience and has the legal knowledge of the different causes of actions that are necessary in achieving a successful case, then it gives you a great feeling of comfort and confidence.

Also, a good attorney who specializes in motorcycle injury cases will know best how to maximize your recovery, know all interested parties to sue or go after to ensure there is plenty of insurance funds to make you whole again, and he or she will also know how to make sure your injury case is properly documented for settlement value. A good lawyer can also help you obtain good medical care if you have no insurance!

Make sure your lawyer has experience by asking how many cases he or she handles in motorcycle injuries in a given year, and whether or not he or she has trial experience – that is, take an injury case all the way to a jury verdict.

CHAPTER 7

WHEN TO HIRE AN EXPERIENCED LAWYER THAT HANDLES CALIFORNIA MOTORCYCLE INJURY CASES

This chapter is listed under *The Motorcycle Injury Defense Strategy* for a reason. The longer you wait to get a consultation from an experienced lawyer handling motorcycle injury cases, the better for the defense, plain and simple.

Consulting with an experienced lawyer with motorcycle injuries is an important first step in the process of resolving your motorcycle injury claim. A consultation with such an attorney not only helps you understand your legal options and rights for you, but also addresses future concerns and legal issues with your entire injury case. As you carefully read through these chapters about the many different legal requirements, and issues involved in a motorcycle injury claim, you will be certain hiring an experienced attorney is a smart move. Simply put, there are too many things that can go wrong when handling a claim on behalf of an injured motorcyclist in California. Before I talk about using an experienced California motorcycle injury lawyer for your injury case, however, let us discuss insurance companies.

Dealing with the Insurance Company in Your Motorcycle Injury Case:

At some point, when a person is injured by a negligent third party (another person not being safe enough to prevent injury), the injured party has to deal with the insurance company through a person known as a claims adjustor. Apart from this aspect, the injured party needs to address questions of damages and liability, including, but not limited to, payment for medical expenses (both future and past), and any other "special damages" surrounding the injuries. At times, this task can be very exhausting and time consuming. The injured party usually deals with the added stress of being injured, obtaining medical care which is time consuming with doctor visits, but also his or her medical progress may be going badly, or it is unknown. The claims adjustors who work for insurance companies are trained professionals who can, at times, take advantage of the situation in order to get the injured party's motorcycle injury claim resolved for as low a monetary value as possible.

Many insurance company claims adjustors have great voices, and they talk to you in a very respectful, and soothing way, in an attempt to gain your trust, and draw information from you about your motorcycle injury claim. This "nice person approach" is oftentimes an attempt by them to gather informal comments and take them out of context to build a case against your motorcycle injury claim. Even in their marketing, insurance companies brand themselves as the "good neighbor," or "are you in good hands?" Remember, because you are the injured party, they will talk to you directly (if you are not represented by experience legal counsel). I had conversations with insurance claims adjustors——who spoke to the injured party——tell me prior to my retention that they believe my injured client is not injured too badly because the injured party recently told him he returned to school or work on a given day. This conclusion is drawn by the claims adjustor without looking at one single piece of medical evidence! When this occurs, I always have to build the foundation for the injuries so the insurance company sets the appropriate settlement reserves on a motorcycle injury case. Otherwise, we have to prepare for a lawsuit and ultimately a jury trial.

An insurance claims adjustor may ask you if they can digitally record your recollection of the motorcycle collision to expedite payment of your injury claim. However, the insurance company representative's goal is always the same: to save the insurance company money by minimizing payment (settlement value) to your motorcycle injury claim. Often times, as I previously noted, the most casual comment you make to an insurance company claims adjustor "may" reduce your motorcycle injury compensation. It is important to keep in mind, the idea of "off the record" does not exist with insurance companies. Something as simple as a polite response——"not too bad"——to a claims adjustor's question to your motorcycle injury claim——"How are you feeling today?"——can turn up as evidence used against you in your motorcycle injury case.

Insurance companies **deny, delay, defend**, or **underpay** motorcycle injury claims all the time. If their insured was reckless in the collision, the insurance company does not tell you that you may have additional damages against their insured for instance: *punitive damages* or *punitive exposure*. The insurance company claims adjustor's goal, often, is to find a way to show that their client (insured) was either *not at fault* or, at a minimum, *partly at fault.* If that is not possible in a motorcycle injury claim, the claims adjustor attempts to move "heaven and earth" to prove that your body sustained no permanent damages or limited medical damages. They may even try to intimidate or confuse you, so that you unwittingly release valid motorcycle injury claims, and waive your legal right to pursue additional financial compensation. Briefly stated, insurance companies do everything in their power to pay as little as possible on your motorcycle injury claim because that is what a business does: a business makes and then guards a profit, and the insurance companies are big businesses with big profits to protect. Also, like a business, insurance companies do not want to pay out full value on a given motorcycle injury claim unless they are forced to pay out full value, plain and simple. Especially, as we already discussed, motorcycle injury cases are unique, and thereby more challenging as they have more leeway to being exploited by the defense.

Is a California Injury Lawyer Who Specializes in Motorcycle Injuries Necessary for Your Case?

You want a motorcycle injury lawyer who is a professional, and who has years of experience dealing with insurance companies with the same injuries as your injury; and has years of experience with the facts of how your motorcycle injury occurred. You also want an experienced lawyer that has jury trial, and not just settlement experience.

Remember, the insurance company's job is to do everything it can to minimize your motorcycle injury claim, and avoid paying fair compensation to cover your past expenses and future medical needs. (See my free book download, ***The 10 Secrets You Need to Know About Your Injury Case, BEFORE You Call A Lawyer,***[2] on my website, **www.blanelaw.com/reports**, to find out how the insurance companies operate as a business.)

In fact, in some motorcycle injury situations, the amount of the insurance adjustor's annual bonus pay *may* be connected to the actual amount of money the adjustor saves the insurance company by offering a lower dollar amount on your motorcycle injury claim. It is recommended that you hire an experienced lawyer that specializes in California motorcycle injury cases to work on your injury claim when the injuries are serious or permanent, or when you have medical bills that cannot be paid or covered under your private health insurance plan, or when you need help finding good doctors to obtain medical treatment.

The Attorney Contingency Fee for a California Motorcycle Injury Case:

Understandably, most folks are worried about hiring a California motorcycle injury lawyer because of the additional expense of doing so; however, most injury cases are handled by experienced lawyers on a contingency basis. A contingency fee agreement is an agreement with a lawyer to defer his or her attorney fee until the case successfully settles or resolves at trial (or at a mediation, or the like). The actual fee is based on a percentage of the recovery obtained by the lawyer through his or her legal talent and efforts. If there is no monetary recovery, then no attorney fee is owed.

Most contingency fees for an adult injury case can range anywhere from twenty-five percent to fifty percent of the gross recovery; but,

2. Mark C. Blane, Esq., ***The Ten Secrets You Need to Know About Your Injury Case, BEFORE You Call a Lawyer***, Word Association Publishers, 2010.

in California, the contingency fee for an injured child, it is capped statutorily at twenty-five percent of the gross recovery,[3] *unless* the attorney did *exceptional* legal work that is approved by a California Superior Court judge.[4] I generally charge a 33% contingency fee on all adult injury cases before filing a lawsuit; 36% after the filing of a lawsuit; and 40% after a lawsuit is filed. For children, I generally charge between 25%-33% of the gross recovery throughout representation.

Many times, in certain serious motorcycle injury cases, it can take years to resolve the case, and the lawyer will spend hundreds of hours on the case before he or she gets paid. To this end, contingency attorney fees allow people of limited financial resources to hire the best legal representation possible. This is very important, because the insurance companies will retain some of the most expensive and experienced defense attorneys to help deny, delay, defend, to try and underpay your motorcycle injury claim.

The Attorney Costs in a California Motorcycle Injury Case are Apart and Separate from the Attorney Contingency Fee:

The attorneys' costs associated with a motorcycle injury claim are a different matter. The term "costs" refers to those expenses that are incurred while investigating the motorcycle injury claim, and prosecuting it in civil court, if necessary. Examples of typical costs include expert fees, court costs (filing lawsuit and service fees), deposition fees, medical record retrieval expenses, and the like.
In California, an attorney is permitted to advance all costs, and then deduct them from the client's gross recovery at the conclu-

3. See *California Family Code Section 6602; California Probate Code Sections 2644, 3601.*
4. See L.A. Super. Ct. Rule 10.79(c)(3). All courts in California consider the time expended and complexity of the case; but, generally, they will only approve a lower than normal percentage——hence, twenty-five percent is usually approved.

sion of the case. This is crucial because it allows the client to hire an attorney without ever having to pay out-of-pocket fees—such fees are paid back to the lawyer only at the time of settlement, or when the verdict from a jury or arbitrator is delivered and settlement funds are received.

Most experienced and reputable lawyers who handle motorcycle injuries agree to advance costs in a case. I do the same for my injured clients. There are some exceptions, of course, depending on the type of motorcycle injury case, and the facts involved.

What a California Lawyer who Specializes in Motorcycle Injuries Can Do for Your Specific Injury Case:

Many people in California simply do not know what an experienced lawyer who specializes in motorcycle injuries can do with their injury case. The following is a list of the types of legal services that a good lawyer is able to successfully provide for your injury case:

- Provide initial, free, and private interview with all injured persons, and discuss all possible legal options and outcomes;

- Educate, assist, and teach the injured person(s) about the California litigation process; what happens after a lawsuit is filed and served, and what timeframes can be expected;

- Obtain, research, read, and analyze all applicable liability insurance policies that may apply (e.g., automotive, homeowners, health, etc.) to see what type of insurance coverage is available to pay for the injured party's damages, such as medical, hospital, and wage loss benefits;

- Arrange, meet, and confer with the injured party's medical doctors, physical therapists, chiropractors, acupuncturists, and other healthcare providers to fully understand the injured party's medical and injury condition.

- Assist the injured client to obtain medical care if he or she is without health insurance;

- Analyze and review any pertinent California legal issues that may negatively (or positively) affect the injured party's motorcycle bodily injury case, such as contributory negligence, assumption of risk, comparative fault, fault of other parties, etc.;

- Draft and file any and all necessary legal claim forms with the at-fault governmental (public) agency. Special rules apply in California if the injured party was injured by a public (governmental) entity;

- Obtain, analyze, and review any and all health insurance or governmental benefit plans to determine whether any money that was spent must be repaid under both federal and California state law.

- Obtain and organize client information (safety certificates, etc.) to argue that the client *was and is a safe motorcyclist.*

- If the insurance company is unable to resolve your injury case, and we need to file a lawsuit, I will prepare and file the lawsuit, and lead the litigation to see if the case will settle during the lawsuit, or ultimately in front of a jury or judge, the final decision makers. I have jury trial experience therefore, I will prepare you every step of the way in the process.

There may be other legal tasks, depending on the facts of the motorcycle injury case, and the injured person's special needs, if any, that I will dutifully perform on the case. The list I have just provided will, at the very least, give the reader some idea of the scope of legal work that may be necessary to successfully pursue and conclude a legal claim on behalf of an injured motorcyclist in the state of California. In the end, it is always best to prepare each injury case, in the very beginning, as if it were to go to trial, and to stand behind this commitment if the insurance company does not make a reasonable offer.

Attorney Mark C. Blane's Legal Representation Process:

All injured persons in a motorcycle collision receive a free and private consultation with me directly. We can meet in person, or online via zoom, skype, or facetime. Or, simply on the phone and we can use email and fax for the paperwork. If meeting in person, we can meet in my law office in San Diego, or we can meet in your home or a local coffee shop. I hold no expectation that a person retains me on our first meeting, and I make sure to let the person know they can think about it.

Each side (potential client and me) "interviews" the other to ensure a good fit for legal representation. Then, questions are asked by the potential client and me, answers are provided, as well as the legal process is fully explained. If I decide to accept a motorcycle injury case, it is done under a written contingency fee, which means I only get paid a fee for my legal services when there is a successful outcome on the case.

After the signed retainer agreement is completed, the following process transpires:

- The client's injury case is opened, and a paralegal is assigned to the specific case. The legal team and I will be the client's main contacts from that point forward. I personally supervise all legal work, and keep the client informed of anything of legal significance on their case. The client will have my personal cell phone number for both calls and text messages, my law office number, my fax number, and my e-mail address. The client is allowed to contact me any time, day and night.

- The legal team is assembled to investigate, and build evidence to support the injured motorcyclist's injury case. In all injury cases, we order the medical records and other official documentation, and we interview any and all witnesses, when necessary.

- A settlement demand is typically drafted, and presented to the at-fault party's insurance offering to resolve the claim without the necessity of litigation (filing a lawsuit in court). This is usually done after any and all medical care is completed. Clients should always be part of every settlement discussion.

- If a settlement is not reached, and after a discussion with the client and obtaining the client's approval, a lawsuit is filed against the responsible parties.

- Additional evidence is gathered in a process known as "discovery" as my law office prepares for trial.

- Court-ordered mediation is likely to occur between the injured motorcyclist and the insurance carrier of the at-fault party in hopes of resolution without the need for trial. Each side, of course, will be represented with lawyers. Sometimes a case may proceed to an agreed arbitration, which is just like a trial, except there is no jury, only a one judge/arbitrator. If this happens or becomes an option on the case, I will discuss it with my client. If mediation or arbitration fails, the motorcycle injury case progresses to a possible settlement conference just prior to trial—and, if that fails, the case moves on to a jury trial in the California Superior Court.

What Items Should You Beware of When Selecting a Lawyer Who Specializes in Motorcycle Injuries?

The following are some warning signs to be aware of when selecting a motorcycle injury lawyer:

- **Beware of large "personal injury mills" which are injury law firms that make their profit through high volume and fast turn over with their injury cases**. The cases are usually handled by paralegals and the attorney only steps in when necessary. One sign is their advertisements are found everywhere around town on freeway signs, buses, trucks and bus benches.

In some cases, the client never meets the attorney at all! Their number one goal is to settle as many cases as fast as they can because they lose money by spending more time on a case and would rather not litigate or go to trial at all. It would serve you well to avoid these large "churn and burn" law firms, as their bottom line can be in conflict with your best interests. If the attorney is too busy to meet with you, evaluate your case, or answer your questions in person, that is a bad sign. And, it usually starts with the law firm sending a "runner" to your house to sign retainer paperwork. The runner is not even a lawyer or paralegal in most cases. It makes one wonder if the lawyer will be able to handle your injury case successfully.

- **Beware of attorneys who make contact with you first, just "out-of-the-blue."** In many cases, this can actually be illegal, not to mention unethical! Sometimes the law firm will know you were in collision by reviewing the public traffic collision reports and send you a letter marked as "legal advertising."

- **Beware of attorneys who promise or guarantee you a specific outcome in your case**. This usually in the form of how much money your case will settle for. Especially when you are not even done with your medical care.

- **Beware of attorneys who do not have experience in handling motorcycle collision cases**. As we discussed in this book, such cases are unique and challenging and have the potential for so many defense tactics. You want an attorney that also has jury trial experience, and not all personal injury lawyers can say they have it!

- **Beware of attorneys who have an endless collection of doctors to whom they will readily refer you, even though you have health insurance for you own doctors**. Generally speaking, these attorneys use the same doctors over and over again in every case, and the doctors get thousands of dollars in fees from the referrals. As a result, at times, the attorney will value his or her relationship with the doctor over you, and your best interest. Furthermore, the insurance companies have computers that keep track of these nefarious relationships, and can use this against your settlement value.

- **Beware of attorneys who try to rush you into signing a retainer agreement**. This behavior does not give you time to review it in detail and ask questions about the retainer. A clear sign that something is not right.

- **Beware of an attorney who has a lot of paralegals**. This can be a sign that you will be passed off to a paralegal, and the lawyer may not even do any work on your case. It is also a good sign that you will be speaking to the paralegals on most matters, and not the lawyer.

- **Beware of general practice attorneys who do more than one area of the law**. As discussed above, the motorcycle injury claim process is a minefield that calls for an experienced attorney who knows how to get you safely to the other side of the minefield. If your attorney does personal injury, criminal and bankruptcy cases etc., it is likely he or she is *spread too thin* to be a focused expert in personal injury law.

PART FOUR: ADDITIONAL INJURY & SAFETY INSIGHTS

CHAPTER 8

FAQ'S REGARDING CALIFORNIA MOTORCYCLE INJURY CASES

Q: WHAT KIND OF MOTORCYCLE INJURY CASES DO YOU NOT ACCEPT?

A: It depends on certain factors that are present.

So, I made the following list:

- **Motorcycle collision injuries where the statute of limitations is about to run out**. Thus, if your case is close to the two-year anniversary of the collision, I may not take it on. There are too many things I am not aware of in order to be effective in my representation.

- **Motorcycle collision cases where there was a prior attorney involved**. Thus, if you had a prior lawyer, there are too many things that I was not in control of from the very beginning, and I generally do not take these cases on.

- **Motorcycle collision cases where there was no injury or very minor injuries**. Thus, if your injury required no medical care, or very little, then that may be a case I cannot take on because it would not be cost-effective for the person to retain me. They would be better off handling the case on their own, or utilizing the California small claims court.

Q. WHAT IS IMPORTANT ABOUT MOTORCYCLE LANE POSITIONS?

A. Lane position is very important to a motorcyclist. As your lane position affects vital aspects to your safety as follows:

- Your ability to see and be seen, it avoids others' blind spots,
- It protects your lane from other drivers,
- It communicates your intentions,
- It helps you avoid wind blasts from other vehicles, and,
- It provides **an escape route!**

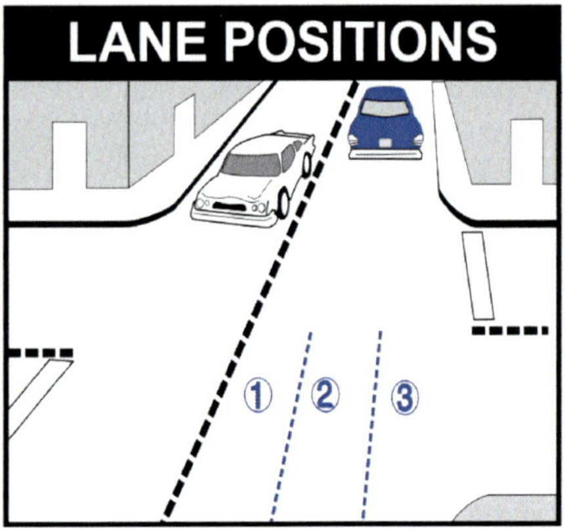

From the California Motorcycle DMV Handbook, pg. 17

In many ways, the size of your motorcycle can work to your advantage, as each traffic lane gives you three paths of travel as indicated in the diagram above. Select the appropriate lane position to maximize your space cushion, and make yourself more visible to others on the roadway.

There is no "best lane position" for motorcyclists as traffic conditions are continually in flux. Change your lane position as traffic conditions dictate. Ride in paths 2 or 3 if vehicles and other potential hazards are on your left side. If you have vehicles on both sides of you, then ride in the center of the lane (path 2). Also, when you ride closer to the center of your lane, it helps keep other vehicles from sharing the lane. Just be aware of any oily or grease build ups in the center of the lane sometimes. You do not want to ride on oily or greasy build ups in the lane.
Also, in case you get injured in a collision, it is best to recollect, to the best of your ability, which lane position you had just before the collision. This could be one of the pieces of evidence that will help your motorcycle injury case.

Q: WHERE ARE MY BLIND SPOTS AS A MOTORCYCLIST?

A: Checking your mirror(s) is not enough, as motorcycles have "blind spots" just like other vehicles.

Before you change lanes, turn your head and check that lane for other vehicles. On a road with several lanes, check the far lane and the one next to you. A driver in the distant lane may drive into the same space you plan to take. Frequent head checks should be part of your normal scanning routine. Only by knowing what is happening all around, can you be fully prepared to deal with any changes on the roadway. Please see diagram below:

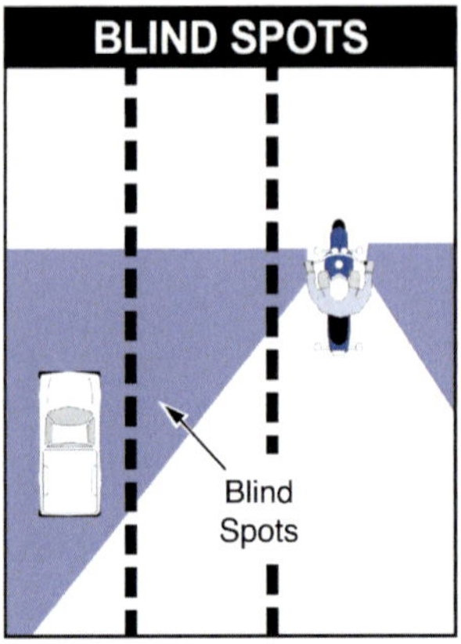

From the California Motorcycle DMV Handbook, pg. 29

Q: WHERE ARE BLIND SPOTS ON OTHER VEHICLES SHARING THE ROAD WITH ME?

A: They are the same for a regular vehicle driver on the roadway, immediately to the left and right side of any vehicle, but a motorcyclist has to be more diligent as they are much smaller and quicker than a regular car making them harder to see.

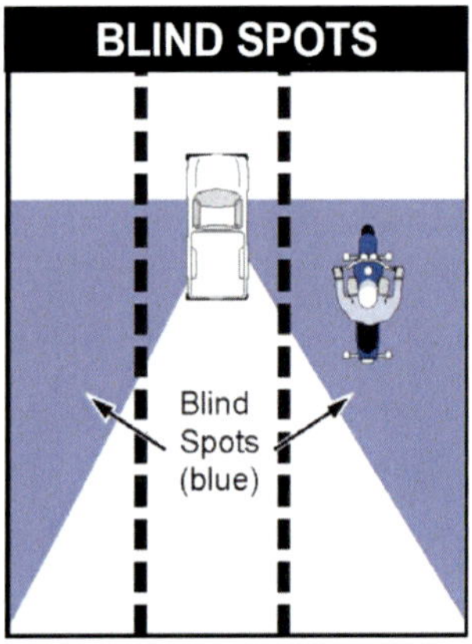

From the California Motorcycle DMV Handbook, pg. 21

The above diagram shows why you should not ride next to a passenger vehicle or truck in other lanes *if you do not have to* because you might be in the driver's blind spot. The driver could change lanes without warning!

I would say changing lanes without warning is a common reason why a preventable motorcycle collision occurs. This is also crucial when you are performing a lane-split maneuver. Only do the lane-split when necessary and under the CHP guidelines documented in this book under Chapter 4. As discussed in this book, lane-splitting is one of the biggest areas an insurance company will play with in any given motorcycle injury claim.

Q: WHAT ARE COMMON TYPE OF COLLISONS IN A CALIFORNIA MOTORCYCLE INJURY?

A: There are many different types of motorcycle collisions that produce injury that I have seen in my law practice over the years, and the following represent some of the most common:

1. Unsafe highway lane switches by vehicles cutting off the motorcyclist. This is by far one of the most common type of collisions (blind spot violations);
2. Unsafe lane turns by vehicles cutting off the motorcyclist or hitting them on the side;
3. Rear-end collisions;
4. U-turns or exits from driveways made unsafely in front of a motorcyclist;
5. Red light runs T-boning the motorcyclist;
6. Car doors opening unexpectedly;

7. Drunk drivers;
8. Speeding and distracted driving;
9. Mechanical failure;
10. Defective roadway design;
11. Road debris; and,
12. Unsafe conduct by motorcycle passenger usually resulting in a single-motorcycle crash.

Understand: Whatever the reason or cause of a motorcycle collision, it always comes down to a *conscious choice*. Someone was either paying full attention to the safety rules of the road, or chose not to. *There is a right way to do things, and there is a wrong way to do things.* This is exactly what we teach our kids.

There is no such thing as "accident." One is never victim of an accident, but rather, a choice made by someone choosing to be unsafe. The defense likes to toy with this and call everything their insured did a *harmless accident*, rather than embracing the decision behavior concept it really is. An experienced lawyer who specializes in motorcycle injuries, will diligently keep this in check on your injury case.

Q: WHAT SHOULD I KNOW ABOUT RIDING AT NIGHT?

A: Riding at night is more dangerous because it is harder for you to see and be seen.

Wear reflective clothing when riding at night. Picking a motorcycle's headlight or taillight out of the other lights is not easy for drivers. To make up for this, you should:

- **Reduce your speed**. Ride even slower than you would during the day, particularly on roads you do not know well. This increases your chances of avoiding a hazard.

- **Increase distance**. Distances are harder to judge at night than during the day. Your eyes rely upon shadows and light contrasts to determine how far away an object is and how fast it is coming. These contrasts are missing or distorted at night. Allow up to a three-second or more following distance to pass and be passed.

- **Use the vehicle ahead**. The headlights of the vehicle ahead can give you a better view of the road than your high beam. Taillights bouncing up and down can alert you to bumps or rough pavement.

- **Use your high beam**. Get all the light you can. Use your high beam whenever you are not following or approaching another vehicle. Be visible. Wear reflective clothing materials when riding at night.

- **Be flexible** about lane position. Change to the lane position that helps you see, be seen, and keep an adequate space cushion.

Q: WHAT KIND OF SETTLEMENT CAN I OBTAIN IN A CALIFORNIA MOTORCYCLE INJURY?

A: Your settlement is divided into a property damage settlement, and a separate bodily injury damage settlement.

For *property damage*, you are entitled to your motorcycle being repaired or full replacement costs (fair market value under a total loss), including anything for out-of-pocket expenses like damaged personal property, towage bills and rental motorcycle/car.

For *bodily injury damage*, you are entitled to your reasonable and necessary medical bills, wage loss, if any, mileage to and from your doctor visits, out-of-pocket medical bills or expenses, all known as "special damages," and pain and suffering damages, also known as "general damages." Your general damages are tied to your medical diagnosis, prognosis, the intensity, duration and frequency of all medical care, and physical impairment, if any.

Q: WHAT IS EXPECTED OF ME WHEN I RIDE MY MOTORCYCLE IN CALIFORNIA?

A: "Safety First" should be your mantra while riding.

Motorcycling requires you to be familiar with the motorcycle, wear the right clothing and helmet, be visible on the roadway by communicating your intentions to other drivers, keep adequate safe space for passing and lane sharing/splitting, be prepared to respond, and be a responsible and safe rider.

Understand: The law requires the above, otherwise it will be used against you later if you are ever involved in a collision. Thus, it is a good idea to go beyond what the DMV requires in terms of motorcycle safety training if you choose to ride. If you are under 21 years of age, you must take the **California Motorcyclist Safety Program (CMSP)** training course. If you are over 21 years of age, you are not required to take the CMSP training course, but are encouraged to take it. Everyone should at least take this course, not only for your own safety, but it can be used as evidence later that you are a *safe motorcyclist* in your legal case.

Q: WHAT CALIFORNIA MOTORCYCLE SAFETY EQUIPMENT LAWS SHOULD I KNOW?

A: California regulates certain physical attributes of your motorcycle as follows:

1. **Functioning headlights**. According to California law, under **California Vehicle Code Section 25650**, every motorcycle during darkness shall be equipped with at least one and not more than two lighted headlamps which will automatically turn on when the engine is started, and which remain lighted as long as the engine is running.

2. **Handle-bar height**. According to California law, under **California Vehicle Code Section 27801(b)**, a person "shall not drive a two-wheel motorcycle that is equipped with handlebars so positioned that the hands of the driver, when upon the grips, are **more than six inches** above his or her shoulder height when sitting astride the seat."

3. **Turn signals**. According to California law, motorcycles are required to have proper working turn signals, both front and rear. However, turn signals are not required on a motorcycle built and first registered prior to January 1, 1973.

4. **Regulation on motorcycle exhaust system.** California Governor, Arnold Schwarzenegger created the **Motorcycle Anti-Tampering Act** in 2010 and it took effect in 2013. It gives law enforcement authority to cite motorcycles with non-compliant exhaust systems. However, the law only applies to 2013 and newer motorcycles and exhaust systems. So, older motorcycles equipped with aftermarket exhaust systems purchased before January 1, 2013, are not affected.

5. **Mirrors.** Motorcycles in California must be equipped with right and left mirrors, per **California Vehicle Code Section 26709**.

6. **Clothing and helmet.** Most collisions occur in broad daylight. Wear brightly colored or reflective clothing to increase your chances of being seen or noticed. Bright orange, red, yellow or green jackets or vests are the best for being seen. Brightly colored helmets can also help others see you. Reflective material on a vest and sides of the helmet will help drivers see you from the side. Remember, your body is ½ of the visible surface area of the rider/motorcycle unit.

Q: WEARING THE RIGHT GEAR – WHAT SHOULD I WEAR WHEN I RIDE?

A: Your riding gear is "right" if it helps to protect you in a collision.

Your riding gear also protects you from sun, rain, wind, insects, noise and highway debris, as well as pavement. It is designed for more than just crash protection as it is like your "second skin" and protects you from sunburn, deafness from the wind, and any kind of debris flying through the air. In any type of collision, you have a far better chance of avoiding serious injury when you wear:

1. **A motorcycle safety helmet approved by the U.S. Department of Transportation (DOT) which is tested on impact strength, positional stability, chin strap strength, and extent of protection overall**. Look for the certification sticker inside the helmet. Make sure the helmet is free of cracks, or loose pads, and choose from a half-shell, ¾ shell or full-face helmet based on personal preference provided it is approved by the DOT. You can also use a Snell Memorial Foundation certification which exceeds the DOT regulations. Brightly colored helmets can also help others see you. Reflective material on a vest and sides of the helmet will help drivers see you from the side. Remember, your body is ½ of the visible surface area of the rider/motorcycle unit.

2. **Face or eye protection.**
3. **Protective apparel (clothing) like leather or long-sleeved jacket, long heavy pants over ankle boots, full fingered leather gloves**. And,
4. **Keep rain gear handy in the event of a weather change.**

Remember, wearing the right safety gear will also help you in your legal case to show you are a *safe and responsible motorcycle rider*. For more details on this, see **Chapter 5**, ***Top Defense Tactics***.

Q: WHY DOES CALIFORNIA FORBID THE USE OF NON-DOT (Dept. Of TRANSPORTATION) APPROVED HELMETS?

A: Simply put, they are not as safe. A non-U.S. DOT compliant helmet generally has very thin liners and protective padding.

These types of helmets lack the strength, size, and ability to protect the rider during a collision. A non-U.S. DOT compliant helmet may look like U.S. compliant helmets and may be sold alongside U.S. DOT compliant helmets. Make sure the U.S. DOT certification is on the helmet you wish to purchase. Non-U.S. DOT compliant helmets may be referred to as novelty helmets, rain bonnets, lids, loophole lids, beanies, or brain buckets.

A U. S. DOT compliant helmet may be decorated by the owner with stick-on items such as decals, Mohawks, Viking horns, etc. and will not affect the safety properties of the helmet. In a collision, regardless of speed, if you are wearing a U.S. DOT compliant motorcycle safety helmet you are three times more likely to survive a head injury than if you are not wearing a U.S. DOT compliant motorcycle safety helmet.

Brightly colored helmets can also help others see you. Reflective material on a vest and sides of the helmet will help drivers see you from the side. Remember, your body is ½ of the visible surface area of the rider/motorcycle unit.

Q: WHAT SHOULD I NOT WEAR WHEN I RIDE?

A: Safety is everything when riding a motorcycle. Thus, you should not wear the following items:

1. **A "used or expired" helmet**. It is common for a motorcyclist to purchase a secondhand motorcycle helmet because a decent helmet can be expensive. But this is a bad practice and should not be done because you have no idea what the helmet has been through. Drops, heavy collisions or expiration is one of many things that could pertain to that helmet, and you only have one healthy brain. The glue and protective gear inside tends to wear out over time because of heat, sweat and continuous wear from someone else;

2. **Scarves**. The debate goes back and forth on whether wearing one while riding a motorcycle is safe. It really depends on the type of scarf you wear. Generally, regular scarves should always be avoided when riding. You need to think about the physics of such clothing at high speeds. If you wear a long enough scarf, it will trail behind you making it possible to catch on something to yank you back. They also tend to undo themselves in a ride, coming in front of your face, or completely fly off onto the windshield of another vehicle around you.

3. **Loose fitted clothing**. You may have seen that most motorcyclist wear tight clothing such as leather or other synthetic material because tight clothing is much safer than loose fitted clothing.

4. **Dark colored clothing**. You should always assume that the drivers around you cannot see you since motorcyclist are much smaller than other vehicles. Brighter colors are safer, especially in the day light. Now, a lot of motorcycle riding gear comes

in black or grey colors, so you may consider using reflectors if you are riding at night. Just simply buy reflector tape and put it where you need to put it.

5. **Half helmets**. Also known as "brain buckets" or "shorty's." See photograph below:

A pair wearing "brain buckets"

I always shudder when I see a motorcyclist wearing a half helmet while out riding. Half helmets only cover the top of a rider's head. The main advantage for them is for the rider to have better visibility and hearing since the helmet does not cover the ears.

Although half helmets are better than no helmet at all, they are in reality not a whole lot better or safer. They will only protect the top part of your head *but nothing surrounding the side of your head or your face.*

Brightly colored helmets can also help others see you. Reflective material on a vest and sides of the helmet will help drivers see you from the side. Remember, your body is ½ of the visible surface area of the rider/motorcycle unit.

6. **Shorts and sandals**. This type of clothing will do nothing to protect your skin leaving it completely exposed to dangers while riding or if you get into a collision. Some people argue long pants rip quickly on the concrete and there is no difference from them and shorts, but you still get a few seconds of added skin protection from long pants that will minimize any road abrasion in case of a collision. These should never be worn while riding, even for a quick ride.

7. **Headphones**. It is against the law to wear headphones while riding a motorcycle or bicycle. **California Vehicle Code Section 27400** expressly states a person cannot operate a motorcycle or bicycle wearing a headset covering, or ear plugs in *both ears*. You must leave one ear open, if you are going to do it. Some people argue that having one ear open gives the feeling of being unbalanced. For safety, you want to hear the traffic noise around you, so it is safer to not wear headphones at all.

8. **Heavy backpack**. Unless you have several compartments in your motorcycle, storage space is very limited. Generally, backpacks are safe to wear while riding, you should not wear them if they are very heavy. Even being in a collision could be dangerous wearing a heavy backpack since the heavy items inside the backpack could hit and injure you. Also, heavy backpacks will make the ride more uncomfortable, and even impact your posture negatively.

Q: WHAT IS THE CALIFORNIA HELMET LAW?

A: Since 1992, California Vehicle Code Section 27803 requires all motorcyclists and passengers to wear a helmet when on a motorcycle, motorize bicycle or motor-driven cycle.

The law goes further with "its teeth" requiring both driver and passenger to wear one. It is illegal for a helmeted passenger to ride with a driver who is not wearing a helmet. Also, a helmeted driver may still get a ticket under California law if a passenger on his or her motorcycle is not wearing a helmet. And, the helmet must fit properly on the head with a chin strap without excessive lateral or vertical movement, per section (e) of the same code.

In 1987, before the California helmet law was passed, 77% of motorcyclist fatalities involved victims under the age of 21, with 69% of those injured over the age of 21.

Brightly colored helmets can also help others see you. Reflective material on a vest and sides of the helmet will help drivers see you from the side. Remember, your body is ½ of the visible surface area of the rider/motorcycle unit.

Q: WHAT ARE THE PENALTIES FOR NOT WEARING A HELMET IN CALIFORNIA WHILE RIDING A MOTORCYCLE?

A: The California Highway Patrol (CHP) has taken the position, supported by California state courts, that breaking the law by riding without a helmet is punishable by a fine.

Others have proposed the violation should be viewed as an "equipment violation" that can be corrected without paying a fine. In reality, law enforcement will pull you over if you are not wearing a helmet, and the law gives the officer discretion as to whether to write you a citation, and the amount that you will be fined. Some officers may issue you a verbal warning, or a low fine, but the law gives them authority to write you a citation for up to $250.00.

Brightly colored helmets can also help others see you. Reflective material on a vest and sides of the helmet will help drivers see you from the side. Remember, your body is ½ of the visible surface area of the rider/motorcycle unit.

Q: DO I HAVE A TIME LIMIT IN WHICH TO BRING A CALIFORNIA MOTORCYCLE INJURY CLAIM?

A: Yes, there exists three very important timelines to be aware of in California to bring a California motorcycle injury claim as follows:

Generally, in California, you have **two years** from the date of injury in which to either settle a bodily injury claim, or have it filed in court. Otherwise, you will forever lose your legal right to sue the at-fault party or parties to recover for bodily injuries. For property damage claims, you have up to **three years** from the date of injury to either have the motorcycle property damage claim settled or filed in court.

However, if you were injured by a city or state government entity, like a city bus or state vehicle, then you have up to **six months** to file your claim with that government entity. If your claim is rejected, then generally you have up to one year to file a lawsuit from the rejection date.

Q: WHO CAN BE SUED IN CALIFORNIA MOTORCYCLE INJURY CLAIM?

A: Depending on the facts, there are many possibilities of who you can sue.

Strategically, your lawyer will want to sue every possible person responsible. The following list some of the most common (possible) defendants (at-fault parties):

1. Obviously, the at-fault driver or drivers that caused the motorcycle collision, and the vehicle owner(s) even if the owner(s) was/were not driving;

2. The employer(s) of the at-fault vehicle driver, or drivers (if the driver was under the scope of his and her employment at the time of the motorcycle collision);

3. The owner(s) of any negligently or illegally parked motor vehicle(s) that led to the collision occurring;

4. If the collision was produced by a defective motorcycle design or malfunction, then the manufacturer or seller of the motorcycle, or if a motorcycle collision leading to injuries involved a defective helmet, then the manufacturer or seller of the helmet;

5. If the motorcycle collision was caused by a faulty vehicle repair, then the repair shop where the vehicle was repaired;

6. If a dangerous condition of a public or private roadway caused the motorcycle collision, then the property owner; and,

7. If the motorcycle collision was caused by the motorcycle passenger, then the passenger can be sued directly. Likewise, the

passenger can sue the motorcycle driver if he or she was at fault.

Q: WHAT IS A *"WHIPLASH"* INJURY IN A MOTORCYCLE CRASH?

A: Whiplash is a slang term for an injury that occurs to the neck after the head has been literally "whipped" either forwards and backwards or sideways after a sudden jolt.

Yes, you can suffer from a whiplash injury on a motorcycle just like you can if you were in another motor vehicle like a car. This occurs regardless if you fall off of your motorcycle or not. But, what really happens bio-mechanically in a "whiplash" injury? To answer this, let's talk about three aspects:

1. **The mechanism of injury**: Were you rear-ended, T-boned, or side-swiped on a motorcycle?
2. **The different types of injuries**: The term "sprain" refers to ligament (tough non-elastic tissue that holds bone to bone) injury and "strain" muscle/tendon (elastic tissues that move our bones) injury. Further, there are three grades of sprain & strains (mild, moderate, and severe). When these tissues are injured, there is usually a loss of movement and neck pain but not arm numbness or pain. When there is nerve injury, there is arm pain, numbness or weakness and generally, this is more serious but usually manageable without the need for surgery. When fractures occur, they can be either stable or unstable and may require surgery or a rigid collar.
3. **The treatment options**: Most whiplash injuries are safely managed by chiropractic or with physical therapy approaches

(fractures are the exception). Studies have shown that early movement (proper motion) produces better results than wearing a collar or, not allowing movement. Therefore, gentle mobilization and manipulation approaches favor a better outcome or result. Prompt treatment is important both medically, and to help protect your legal interests in a motorcycle collision!

Q: WHAT ARE THE DIFFERENCES BETWEEN A "SOFT TISSUE" INJURY & A "HARD TISSUE INJURY?":

A: First, one must understand the two classes of tissue found in the human body: Bone, and Soft Tissue.

Every tissue in the body, apart from bones, such as muscles, tendons, and ligaments are considered "soft tissue." A soft tissue injury is an injury to ligaments (known as a sprain), and to muscles and tendons (known as strain). For example, a neck sprain/strain is generally known as a "whiplash soft tissue injury."

In contrast, hard tissue injuries relate to injuries to the bone like fractures, and they tend to heal better with no motion (physical therapy) which is why hard casts are often used in treating them. Soft tissue injuries, on the other hand, tend to heal better with proper motion which is why they respond well to physical therapy and chiropractic.

Bones tend to take longer to heal because the blood supply is lower compared to soft tissue injuries which have potential to heal quicker. Bone breaks tend to heal stronger than they were before the break, but not so for soft tissue injuries which almost never heal back as they were before. Soft tissue injuries cause scar tissue to build up, and they need to be treated right away with proper motion. This will help to prevent the scar tissue causing stagnation of the blood supply to joints of the spine, or body.

Q: WHAT SHOULD I KNOW ABOUT CALIFORNIA MOTORCYCLE PASSENGER LAWS?

A: You may only ride with a passenger on your motorcycle if it is equipped with a designated passenger seat, and passenger footrests.

California, like most other states, does not dictate an age requirement for motorcycle passengers as long as the driver is a California licensed motorcyclist. However, children passengers must be tall enough for their feet to reach the designated passenger footrests, and they must wear helmets, like any other passenger. If you unsafely ride with a child that is too young or small to ride as a motorcycle passenger, you may face child endangerment charges.

Q: WHAT SHOULD I KNOW ABOUT PARKED VEHICLES WHEN RIDING MY MOTORCYCLE?

A: BE WATCHFUL, as they can be a potential hazard!

When passing parked vehicles, stay toward the left portion of your lane of travel. This way, you can avoid any potential problems caused by inattentive drivers or passengers opening their doors on you, or people stepping from between the parked vehicles in front of you. If, however, oncoming traffic is present, it is usually best to remain in the center portion of the lane to maximize the space around you.

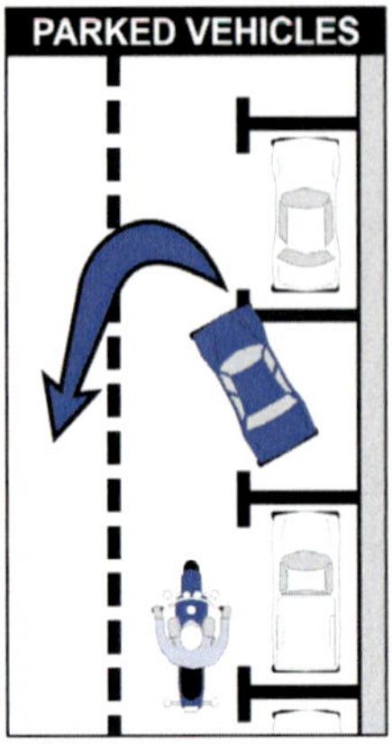

From California Motorcycle DMV Handbook, pg. 26

A bigger problem can occur if a driver pulls away from the curb without checking for on-coming traffic (you) from behind. Even if the driver looks, he or she may still fail to see you coming! In either event, the driver might enter your path of travel, which would not be good. So, slow down or change lanes completely to make enough space for someone to enter.

Vehicles making a sudden U-turn are the most dangerous! This happens all the time, and I see it in my law practice without question. They may cut you off 100%, blocking the entire roadway and leaving you with no place to ride. Since you are not going to be able to predict what exactly a driver will do, you can slow down and try to get the driver's attention by blowing your motorcycle horn and continue forward with extreme caution.

Q: WHAT DO I NEED TO KNOW ABOUT RIDING MOTORCYCLES IN GROUPS IN CALIFORNIA?

A: If you ride with others, do it in a way that promotes safety and does not interfere with the flow of traffic.

Assign a lead and a drag (tail) rider. Both riders should be experienced and familiar with group riding. **California Vehicle Code §21461** requires all vehicles to observe official traffic control devices before entering or crossing the highway. When riders travel in groups and approach an intersection with a stop sign or traffic light, the riders must obey the traffic control devices.

Keep the Group Small: Small groups make it easier and safer for other drivers to get around them. A small number is not separated as easily by traffic or red lights. Remember, some riders will not always be hurrying to catch up. If your group is larger than four or five riders, divide it into two or more smaller groups.

Keep the Group Together:

- **Brief**. Perform a pre-ride overview of the route, hand signals for single-file formation and what to do if a hazard is encountered.
- **Plan**. The leader should look ahead for changes and signal early so there is plenty of time for everyone to follow. Start lane changes early to permit everyone to complete the lane change safely.
- **Put beginners up front**. Place inexperienced riders behind the leader so the more experienced riders can watch them.
- **Monitor those behind**. Let the last rider set the pace. Use your mirror(s) to keep an eye on the rider behind. If a rider falls behind, everyone should slow down a little to stay together.
- **Know the route**. Make sure everyone knows the route. Plan frequent stops on long rides.

Keep Your Distance: Maintain close ranks, but at the same time keep a safe distance to allow each rider in the group time and space to react to hazards. A close group takes up less space on the highway, is easier to see, and is less likely to be separated. However, this formation must be done properly.

- **Do not pair up.** Never operate directly alongside another rider (even though television media has shown it being okay to do). There is no place to go to avoid a vehicle or a hazard on the road. You should wait until you are both stopped to talk. The way they showed it in the hit TV show "CHiPs" and, later the 2017 movie, is discouraged!

Still shot from the 2017 CHiPs (film)

- **Staggered formation.** This is the best way to keep ranks close and maintain an adequate space cushion. **The leader rides in the left portion of the lane** while the second rider stays one second behind in the right portion of the lane. A third rider rides in the left portion of the lane two seconds behind the first rider. The fourth rider keeps a two-second distance behind the second rider. This formation keeps the group close and permits each rider a safe distance from others ahead, behind, and to the sides.

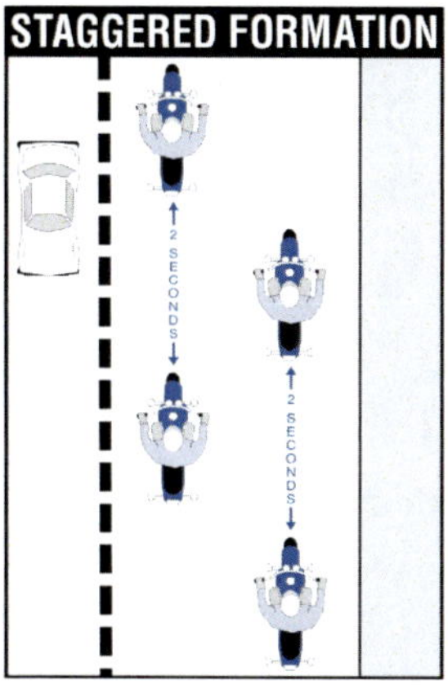

From the California Motorcycle DMV Handbook, pg. 42

- **Passing in formation**. Riders in a staggered formation should pass one at a time.
    - First, the lead rider pulls out and passes when safe. After passing, the leader returns to the left portion of the lane and continues riding at "passing speed" to open room for the next rider.
    - After the first rider passes safely, the second rider moves up to the left portion of the lane and watches for a safe chance to pass. After passing, this rider returns to the right portion of the lane and opens up room for the next rider.
    - Some people suggest the leader should move to the right portion of the lane after passing a vehicle. This is not a good idea. It encourages the second rider to pass and return to the lane before there is a large enough space cushion in

front of the passed vehicle. It is simpler and safer to wait until there is enough room ahead of the passed vehicle to allow each rider to move into the same position held before the pass.

- **Single-file formation.** Move into a single-file formation when riding curves, turning, and entering or leaving a highway.

Q: HOW CAN I AVOID "FLYING OBJECTS" WHEN RIDING MY MOTORCYCLE?

A: From time to time riders are struck by insects, cigarettes thrown from vehicles, or pebbles kicked up by the tires of the vehicle ahead.

Avoid following closely behind dump trucks, waste management vehicles, livestock haulers, agricultural vehicles, construction vehicles, or any vehicle towing or hauling items. Debris such as hay, trash, tree limbs, and other loose items being hauled can fall from the vehicles placing you in an unavoidably dangerous situation. If you are wearing face protection, it might get smeared or cracked, making it difficult to see. Without face protection, an object could hit you in the eye, face, or mouth. Whatever happens, keep your eyes on the road, and your hands on the handlebars. When safe, pull off the road and repair the damage.

Q: WHAT SHOULD I KNOW ABOUT CARRYING PASSENGERS AND CARGO?

A: Only experienced riders should carry passengers or large loads.

The extra weight changes the way the motorcycle handles, balances, speeds up, and slows down. Before taking a passenger or a heavy load on the street, practice away from traffic. Even if your passenger is a motor- cycle rider, provide complete instructions before you start. Tell your passenger to:

- Get on the motorcycle only after you start the engine.
- Sit as far forward as possible without crowding you.
- Hold firmly to your waist, hips, or belt.
- Keep both feet on the footrests, even when stopped.
- Keep legs away from the muffler(s), belts, chains, or moving parts.
- Stay directly behind you leaning as you lean and looking over your shoulder in the direction of the turn.
- Avoid unnecessary talk or motion. The motorcycle will sway with the passenger's movement.

Also, tell your passenger to tighten his or her hold when you:

- Approach surface problems.
- Are about to start from a stop.
- Warn you will make a sudden move.

Your motorcycle will respond more slowly with a passenger. The heavier your passenger, the longer it will take to slow down, stop, and speed up, especially on a light-duty motorcycle. Your braking distance will increase due to the added weight.

- Ride a little slower, especially when taking curves, corners, or bumps.

- Begin slowing sooner as you approach a stop.
- Open up a larger cushion of space ahead and to the sides.
- Wait for larger gaps to cross, enter, or merge with traffic.

Warn your passenger of these special conditions: starting, stopping quickly, turning sharply, or riding over bumps. Turn your head slightly to make yourself understood, but keep your eyes on the road ahead.

Q: WHAT ARE SOME TIPS TO BATTLE FATIGUE WHILE RIDING A MOTORCYCLE?

A: Riding a motorcycle is more tiring than driving a vehicle, especially on a long trip.

Avoid riding when tired. Fatigue can affect your control of the motorcycle. Keep in mind the following:

- **Limit your distance**. Experienced riders seldom ride more than about six hours a day.
- **Take frequent rest breaks**. Stop and get off the motorcycle at least every two hours.
- **Do not drink alcohol or use drugs.** Artificial stimulants often result in extreme fatigue or depression as they start to wear off. You will not be able to concentrate on the task at hand.

Q: WHAT IS CALIFORNIA LAW WITH ALCOHOL AND RIDING A MOTOCYCLE?

A: Obviously, it is illegal, and it is divided into "two different tiers," depending on your age, in California.

In California, it is illegal for a person under 21 years old to drive with a Blood Alcohol Content (BAC) of 0.01% or above; for people under 21 years old, there is ZERO tolerance for alcohol use. It is illegal for a person 21 years old or older to drive with a BAC of 0.08% or above. It does not matter how sober you may look or act; a breath or blood test is what determines whether you are riding legally or illegally.

NOTE: The *California Driver Handbook* (DL 600) has additional information regarding driving under the influence (DUI) of alcohol and/or drugs. Law enforcement is being stepped up across the country in response to the senseless deaths and injuries caused by drinking drivers and riders.

Minimize the Risks

Minimize the risks of drinking and riding by following the steps below:

- **Do not drink.** Once you start drinking, your resistance becomes weaker. ***Choose to become a person who simply does not drink at all.*** In the end, it kills your brain cells, impairs your good judgment and thus, *nothing good comes from alcohol drinking.* Finally, it can set a bad example for children who look up to adults as leaders.
- **Do not ride.** If you are or have been drinking, **do not** ride your motorcycle.

Q: WHAT SHOULD I KNOW ABOUT BRAKING MY MOTORCYCLE?

A: Your motorcycle has two brakes: one for the front wheel and one for the rear wheel, and as such, you should be aware of the following:

When making a normal, nonemergency stop, use both brakes at the same time and downshift. The front brake has more stopping power, providing three-quarters of your total stopping power. The front brake is safe to use when used properly. **REMEMBER**:

- Use both brakes every time you slow or stop. Using both brakes for "normal" stops helps you develop the proper habit and skill of using both brakes correctly, which you may need in an emergency. Squeeze the front brake and press down on the rear brake. Grabbing at the front brake or jamming down on the rear brake can cause the brakes to lock and result in control problems.

- If you know the technique, using both brakes in a turn is possible, although it should be done very carefully. When you lean the motorcycle, some of the traction is used for cornering and less traction is available for stopping. A skid can occur if you apply too much brake. Also, using the front brake incorrectly on a slippery surface may be hazardous. Use caution and gently squeeze the brake lever, never "grab" it.

- Some motorcycles have integrated braking systems that link the front and rear brakes together when you apply the rear brake pedal (consult your owner's manual).

Q: HOW CAN I INCREASE MY VISIBILITY ON MY MOTORCYCLE?

A: There are several things you can do to increase your visibilty, and this should be your goal every time you ride your motorcycle.

In collisions with motorcyclists, drivers often say that they never saw the motorcycle. From ahead or behind, a motorcycle's outline is much smaller than a passenger vehicle's, and can easily not get spotted on the highway. Also, it is hard to see something you are not looking for, and most drivers are not looking for motorcycles. More likely, they are looking through the skinny, two-wheeled silhouette in search of vehicles that may pose a problem to them.

Even if a driver sees you coming, does not mean you are not necessarily safe. Smaller vehicles appear farther away and seem to be traveling slower than they actually are. It is common for drivers to pull out in front of motorcyclists, thinking they have plenty of time. Too often, they are wrong. However, you can do many things to make it easier for others to recognize you and your motorcycle. ***Clothing:*** Most collisions occur in broad daylight. Wear brightly colored or reflective clothing to increase your chances of being seen. Bright orange, red, yellow, or green jackets or vests are the best for being seen. Brightly colored helmets can also help others see you. Reflective material on a vest and on the sides of the helmet will help drivers see you from the side. Reflective material can also be a big help for drivers com-ing toward you or from behind. Remember, your body is half of the visible surface area of the rider/motorcycle unit.

Headlight: The best way to help others see your motorcycle is to **always keep the headlight and, if equipped, running lights on**. A motorcycle with its light on is twice as likely to be noticed. Using your high beam during the day and at night increases the chances that oncoming drivers will see you. Use your high beam when it is legal and safe to do so. When it is foggy, use the low beam.

Q: WHAT ARE 5 THINGS I CAN DO TO BE SAFER WHILE I RIDE MY MOTORCYCLE?

A: You can properly use turning signals, brake lights, mirrors, head checks, and your horn.

Turn Signals: With turning signals, due to a rider's added vulnerability, turn signals are even more important. Use them anytime you plan to change lanes or turn. Signal your left or right turn during the last 100 feet before reaching the turning point. At highway speeds, it is best to signal at least five seconds before changing lanes. Use your turn signals even when you think no one else is around. Your turn signals also make you easier to see. If bright sunlight makes your turn signal lights hard to see, use hand signals. When you enter a freeway, drivers approaching from behind are more likely to see your turn signal blinking and make room for you.

Brake Light: Your motorcycle's brake light is usually not as noticeable as a vehicle's, especially when the taillight is on. If the situation permits, help others notice you by flashing your brake light before you slow down. It is especially important to flash your brake light before you slow:

- For a tight, fast turn off a highspeed highway.
- Where others may not expect it (in the middle of a block or at an alley).

If you are being tailgated, it is a good idea to flash your brake light before you slow.

Using Your Mirrors: While it is most important to know what is happening ahead, you cannot ignore situations behind you. Traffic conditions change quickly. To make safe decisions about how to handle trouble ahead, you must know what is going on around you. Frequent mirror checks should be part of your normal searching routine. Especially when you are stopped at an intersection, before you change lanes, and before you slow down.

Head Checks: Checking your mirror(s) is not enough. Motorcycles have "blind spots" just like other vehicles. Before you change lanes, turn your head and check that lane for other vehicles.

Horn: Be ready to use your horn to get someone's attention quickly. In an emergency, press the horn button loud and long. Be ready to stop or swerve away from the danger. Remember, a motorcycle's horn is not as loud as other vehicles', so use it, but don't rely on it.

Q: WHAT ARE SOME "COLLISION AVOIDANCE" TIPS WHILE RIDING MY MOTORCYCLE?

A: You should know when and how to stop or swerve.

No matter how careful you are, there will be times when you find yourself in a tight spot. Your chances of getting out safely depend on your ability to react quickly and properly. Often, a collision occurs because a motorcycle rider is not prepared or skilled in collision-avoidance maneuvers. As mentioned, two critical skills in avoiding a collision are knowing ***when and how to stop or swerve***. Keep in mind, you cannot always stop quickly to avoid an obstacle.

You must also be able to swerve around an obstacle. Most collisions involve riders who:

- Under-brake the front tire and over-brake the rear.
- Do not separate braking from swerving, or do not choose to swerve when it is appropriate.

Q: WHAT DO I NEED TO KNOW ABOUT "QUICK STOPS" WHILE RIDING MY MOTORCYCLE?

A: To stop quickly, apply both brakes at the same time, and do not be shy about using the front brake, but do not "grab" it either.

Squeeze the brake lever firmly with continuing steady pressure. If the front wheel locks, release the front brake immediately and then reapply it firmly. At the same time, press down on the rear brake. If you accidentally lock the rear brake on a good traction surface, you can keep it locked until you have completely stopped. **NOTE:** Even with a locked rear wheel, you can control the motorcycle on a straightaway if it is upright and going in a straight line. **Always use both brakes at the same time to stop.** The front brake can provide three-quarters of your stopping power.

If you must stop quickly while turning or riding a curve, the best technique is to straighten the motorcycle first and then brake. However, it may not always be possible to straighten the motorcycle, and then stop. If you must brake while leaning, apply the brakes lightly and reduce the throttle. As you slow, reduce your lean angle and apply more brake pressure until the motorcycle is straight and maximum brake pressure is possible. Then in the last few feet of stopping, you should "straighten" the handlebars. The motorcycle should now be straight up and in balance.

Q: WHAT DO I NEED TO KNOW ABOUT "SWERVING OR TURNING QUICKLY" WHILE RIDING MY MOTORCYCLE?

A: Sometimes you may not have enough room to stop, even if you use both brakes properly, as an object might appear suddenly in your path or the vehicle ahead might stop abruptly.

The only way to avoid a collision may be to turn quickly or swerve around it. A swerve is any sudden change in direction. It can be two quick turns, or a rapid shift to the side. To swerve, apply a small amount of hand pressure to the handle grip on the side of your intended direction of escape. This causes the motorcycle to lean quickly. The sharper the turn(s), the more the motorcycle must lean.

Keep your body upright and allow the motorcycle to lean in the direction of the turn. Keep your knees pressed against the tank and your feet solidly on the footrests. Let the motorcycle move underneath you. Make your escape route the target of your vision. Press on the opposite handle grip once you clear the obstacle and are ready to return to your original direction of travel. To swerve to the left, press the left handle grip, then press the right to recover. To swerve to the right, press right, then left. Then press the left or right handle grip to recover.

RESOURCES

The California Motorcycle DMV Handbook

This is the comprehensive California Rule Book on motorcycle riding. You will need it when you study, and re-study for your motorcycle license. Definitely keep a hard-bound copy or PDF copy of this handbook containing all the traffic rules for riding your motorcycle. You can grab a free PDF copy online at the following web address: **https://www.dmv.ca.gov/portal/uploads/2020/03/dl665.pdf**

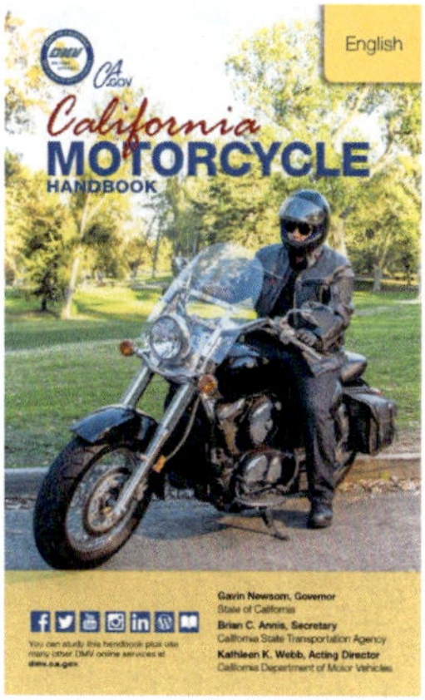

The California Motorcyclist Safety Program (CMSP)

The California Highway Patrol (CHP) is statutorily authorized to be responsible for California's motorcyclist safety and training program. According to **California Vehicle Code Sections 2930-**

2935, the CHP administers the CMSP through a primary contractor, currently, as of 2020, Total Control Training, Inc. As of 2019, over 1,200,000 motorcycle riders have received training at one of the CMSP's many training sites since the program began in July 1987. You can contact the CMSP at **1-877-RIDE-411** or go to **http://cmsp.msi5.com/mapping/** to find a CMSP training center near you!

Motorcycle Safety Foundation (MSF)

Founded in 1973 in Irvine, California, the MSF is internationally recognized as the developer of the comprehensive, research-based, Rider Education and Training System (RETS). RETS promotes lifelong learning for motorcyclists and continuous professional development for certified Rider Coaches and other trainers. MSF also participates in government relations, safety research, public awareness campaigns and the provision of technical assistance to state training and licensing programs. They can be contacted at **800.446.9227**, or via email at **msf@msf-usa.org** or check out their website at **www.msf-usa.org**.

Proficient Motorcycling: The Ultimate Guide to Riding Well, by David L. Hugh, (2008)

This book commands great respect for being one of the best books out there on motorcycle safety ever written. As of the date of this riding, it boasts 644 great reviews on amazon. This book is a "must read" for anyone who is riding a motorcycle.

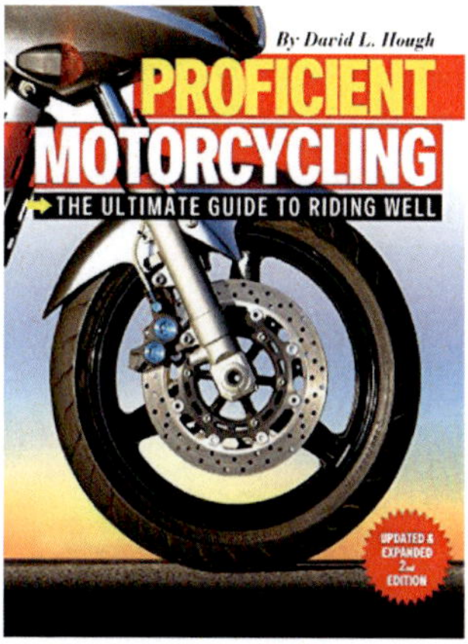

ABOUT THE AUTHOR

California Trial Lawyer Mark C. Blane

www.BlaneLaw.com

California trial lawyer, Mark C. Blane, Esq. is a solo-practicing attorney, and legal author, who specializes in personal injury law in San Diego, California, since 1999. He represents people in southern California who have been injured by the negligence (not being safe enough to prevent harm) of others due to:

- Defective products,
- Automobile, motorcycle, bicycle, pedestrian accidents,
- Slip/trip and falls,
- Dog bites, and animal attacks,

- Wrongful death and,
- Other accidents that have caused catastrophic loss.

He finds himself against some of the largest insurance companies in the United States, in addition to some of the most respected defense law firms in California.

He has handled many injured motorcycle cases over the years which has allowed him to carve out "how and why" the defense likes to exploit these types of injury cases, when possible. This book shares secrets with you developed over years of handling motorcycle collision cases.

He is also a 2017 Masters Graduate of the **Keenan Trial Institute** in Atlanta, Georgia where he honed his skills as a trial lawyer under the philosophy and teachings of the Trial Institute's founder, the legendary trial lawyer, Don Keenan. He has recovered multiple millions of dollars of compensation on behalf of his injured clients since 1999.

He recognized early in his career that he wanted to represent the people instead of corporate interests. He enjoys the strategy and tactics in the courtroom, and understands the necessity of having jury trials available when needed to right the wrongs of those injured by the unsafe and preventable conduct of others. He further understands that not every injury case needs a lawyer, but every injury case, no matter how minor, should be discussed with good legal counsel. The initial consult he provides is always free of charge, and he works exclusively on a contingency-fee basis with all of his cases. This means that if he accepts and works on an injury case, he only charges a fee when he successfully resolves

the case—otherwise, there is no charge for his legal services. Thus, there is no financial risk to the client.
His San Diego law office primarily consists of a team of paralegals, and one *Of Counsel* attorney member. He likes keeping his legal team small, and approachable so he can make sure his clients get his personal attention.

When he is not practicing injury law, you can find him reading, working out (calisthenics, weights and yoga), or running on San Diego's many beaches or beautiful hiking trails. You can reach him anytime at **619.813.7955** or via email at **mark@blanelaw.com**, and you can check him out online at **www.blanelaw.com**, and at most popular social media platforms.

WA

Made in United States
Orlando, FL
22 October 2026

89528902R00100